As Iron Sl

An Adventure in Building
Gentlemanly Character

G. Andrew Meschter

1

Dedication

This book is dedicated to John Seel, a former prep-school headmaster who understands the problems and possibilities facing young men.

Contents

Foreword

Can Masculinity Be Saved?

There is a lot of justified complaining about "toxic masculinity" today. Its evidence is everywhere. This has created a kind of defensive paralysis in men. At a time of gender confusion, the #metoo movement, mass incarceration in our prison system, the absence of noble male role models, the perception of a misogynist President, and delayed maturation of youth, it is a hard time to be male.

The notorious Gillette ad asked, "How can a man be the best that he can be?" This book is a personal answer to that question from the standpoint of being a gentleman.

Culturally, this is contested terrain. The premise of this book is that the antidote to the feminist critique of patriarchy is not the feminization of men but a return to genuine ennobling masculinity. As a personal exploration and an historical examination of the gentleman virtues, this book is timely and long overdue.

Other voices in this area include David Brooks and Van Jones. As a social scientist student of the millennial generation, preparatory school headmaster, crew coach, father of two millennial boys, and grandparent, I have spent many years concerned about the development of men.

This book is a timely response to our cultural moment. Literary critic Kenneth Burke writes that all documents are a situation strategy: an answering to a larger cultural question. So too is this book. This memoir may not have all the answers, but it is a compelling onramp to a needed conversation among men. You will enter into this conversation not with simplistic platitudes, psychological abstractions, or know-it-all masculine confidence, but through the prism of struggle, honesty, and vulnerability. It is a book for men by a manly man without apology. It made me a better man in the reading. This is a must read for my own and the next generation.

John Seel, Ph.D.
Erdenheim Farm
Lafayette Hill, Pennsylvania

America Was Founded by Gentlemen

If I were an Englishman writing this book a few generations ago, I'd have to kick things off with some nonsense about how a true gentleman never speaks about being a gentleman. Then I'd have to quickly apologize for writing in the first person, because personal pronouns are traditionally considered bad form. But it's 2019, and on this side of the Atlantic, we can afford to be somewhat brash.

This book is about the old-school English idea of the gentleman as explored by a (somewhat) modern American. We'll discuss how the idea of the gentleman reconciles two facets of human character development which at first glance seem mutually exclusive: a) the urge to become the strongest and most excellent person you can possibly be, while b) continually learning to put others above yourself.

The best way to accomplish these twin aims is to learn from people who challenge, inspire, and even annoy you. Our cue for this comes from a biblical phrase in Proverbs 27:17 (NIV) which states "As iron sharpens iron, so one person sharpens another."

We take this a step further by suggesting that people tend to sharpen each other best when they spend time together in *communities* that face *adversity* together, where internal *honor* codes make it difficult

9

to opt out. Such groups would include small-town volunteer fire companies, elite boarding schools, dodgy business start-ups, military units, sports teams, college fraternities, and even marriages . . . to name but a few.

If this story has a target audience, it's young men in their late teens and early twenties (the age I was when experiencing most of the things here described). The age, in other words, when testosterone runs highest, when life still seems up for grabs, and when guys are most likely to take risks. Of course, it's also written for everyone else.

Recently, young men have been castigated in the media as an at-risk group in society whose cultural norms foster "toxic masculinity." A quick internet search describes toxic masculinity as a "narrow and repressive description of manhood, designating manhood as defined by violence, sex, status and aggression. It's the cultural ideal of manliness, where strength is everything while emotions are a weakness..."[1] This definition is quite helpful for the theme of this book. It conveniently encapsulates exactly what gentlemanly character was invented to address.

---

[1] https://www.tolerance.org/magazine/what-we-mean-when-we-say-toxic-masculinity

Childhood Interest in this Topic

My interest in the idea of the gentleman goes back to childhood. In a sense, I've wrestled with it my whole life. It probably all stems from where I was born—in exurban Philadelphia within five or ten miles of where my ancestors first settled in the 1700s.

When you grow up where local houses pre-date the Revolution, within easy driving distance of Valley Forge Park, Independence Hall, the Liberty Bell, countless places where George Washington may or may not have slept, battlefield markers at Trenton and Princeton, and the ancient streets of Germantown and Society Hill, it's easy to feel haunted by the Founding Fathers.

You learn from an early age about Washington, Lafayette, Franklin, Jefferson, Hamilton, Muhlenberg, and many others and you admire how well educated, well-traveled, brave, innovative, collaborative, and accomplished they all were. And you learn that they shared an *honor code* as colonial subjects who considered themselves British gentlemen as well as Americans. Eventually, you start to see them as role models for earthly success.

But as I said, I originally had a "wrestling match" with the idea of being a gentleman. As a young kid, whenever the term "gentleman" cropped up, it was from adults trying to get me to behave in ways I didn't want to: when Mom wanted me to share with my sisters, when Dad spent hours taking me to task about character flaws, when Mom-Mom Meschter wanted me to eat politely at dinner and send thank-you notes, or when Mrs. Stavisky chided me for coming in from third-grade recess covered in mud.

In short, my awareness of gentlemanly behavior came through a combination of "carrot and stick." Adults in authority swung the sticks (figuratively, of course) by doing what they could to keep me in line. The carrots came as it later dawned on me that my favorite role models (living, dead, and fictional)— the characters I most wanted to be like—were all surprisingly gentlemanly. Gentility was the one thing my heroes all seemed to have in common.

My dad, grandfathers, and other family members were early behavioral models of course. Dad the scrupulous small-town business man busy with local boards whose calm demeanor poured oil on the waters whenever conflicts arose, Pop-Pop Dell the ex-navy pilot who still spoke in clipped war-time speech and flew planes from Perkiomen Valley Airport, or Kyrel Meschter the relative who did something at Girard, an old Philadelphia bank.

Certain teachers in school were also models. Three of my favorites, Mr. Zeigler, Mr. Krieger, and Mr. Keenan were the ones I most initially disliked (an early introduction to the life-long iron-sharpening-iron principle). Then came political figures I read about like Teddy Roosevelt, John F. Kennedy, and George Washington who used their privileges to serve others with panache in public life. Certain businessmen appeared on the radar who also seemed gentlemanly, such as Drew Lewis (a local hero), John Bogle of Vanguard fame, advertising man David Ogilvy, and J. P. Morgan (who at the 1912 Pujo Hearings insisted that investment banking was based on raw personal *character* and who famously sought to hire "gentlemen with brains").

On top of all that, my fictional heroes always seemed gentlemanly. They were all tough but swank. Robin Hood (an outlaw nobleman stealing for the poor), James Bond (jujitsu in Savile Row suits), Indiana Jones (a professor swinging from vines), Sherlock Holmes (encyclopedic knowledge, able to bend iron bars with his bare hands), Tarzan (nobleman turned noble savage)—not to mention John Buchan's Richard Hannay and Sandy Arbuthnot, Emma Orczy's *The Scarlet Pimpernel*, or Erskine Childers's intrepid yachtsmen in *The Riddle of the Sands*. This list of fictional heroes could go on and on.

In every case these characters (living and imaginary) were, to repeat J. P. Morgan's phrase, "gentlemen with brains." In various ways each man swung a big line, took big risks, and embraced conflict with an honor code rooted in a muddy mix of Christian morality and unwritten British-inspired class mores.

As I advanced through high school and college, this interest in being an *American gentleman*—and not just an ordinary American—was mainly driven by a feeling that our nation was *founded* by gentlemen.

The American Founders were Gentlemen

That's right, the guys in powdered wigs and knee britches who pledged their lives, fortunes, and "Sacred Honor" to sign the Declaration of Independence in 1776 and who framed the US Constitution in 1789 were members of a colonial "ruling class" (i.e. "movers and shakers") who weren't just normal folks.

Writing about them, Alexis de Tocqueville said "When the American Revolution declared itself, remarkable men came forward in droves. In those days, public opinion gave direction to their wills, but did not tyrannize them. The famous men of their day freely took part in the intellectual movement of their time yet possessed a grandeur all their own. Their brilliance, rather than being borrowed from the nation, spilled over into it."[2]

These Founders were products of iron sharpening iron. They came from two competing backgrounds that remain in healthy conflict today. That is, they represented an ancient struggle between new and old power. Some of them were established (old money) people, expensively educated in Britain, who (using an old baseball analogy) were "born on third base." Others were ambitious newcomers with hunger, brains, and talent (cue "Eye of the Tiger") who wanted a say in running things that the colonial system would have never granted them.

---

[2] Alexis de Tocqueville, *Democracy in America* (Library of America, New York, 2004).

Take George Washington for example. For all his fox-hunting, ballroom dancing, and rich local connections, Washington worked his way up from sparse beginnings. Had British bureaucracy given young Washington the officer's commission he yearned for in the regular army, he might never have fought the redcoats at Bunker Hill later in life.[3] That English culture denied men like Washington the chance to enter the establishment said something of its lack of ability to absorb the best and brightest; that Britain's empire permitted such men of talent to become wealthy and powerful in the first place said something of its flexibility and ability to grow from within.

This yin-yang dynamic between absorbing new talent while keeping it in check has always been part of the alchemy of what it means to be a gentleman.

A Blending of Egalitarian and Elite

As English speakers, the Founders came from a culture that had been walking a tightrope between equality and hierarchy for centuries. In his essay "English Traits" Ralph Waldo Emerson attributed this dichotomy to an ancient tug-of-war between democratic Saxons and aristocratic Normans.[4] There's a sense that these two cultures have been duking it out in the Anglophone world for centuries:

---

[3] Ron Chernow, *Washington: A Life* (Penguin Press, New York, 2010).

[4] Ralph Waldo Emerson, "English Traits: Ability," *Emerson: Essays and Lectures* (Library of America, New York, 1983).

through the Magna Carta (nobles versus royals), the English Civil War (gentry versus nobles), the American Revolution (yeomanry versus gentry), the US Civil War (freedom versus slavery).

In every instance however, ladies and gentlemen stand out as people who can straddle this divide. With aplomb they're able to *blend* these conflicting halves—egalitarian and elite—in their own characters into a polite, pragmatic, balanced whole.

An early role model for this was William of Wykeham, who founded New College at Oxford in 1379. By adopting the motto "Manners makyth man," Wykeham claimed that manners determined human value, and not just wealth and birth. The American Founders carried this torch when they framed the US Constitution and made equal room for old-world gentility (the mores of people in power who *allow* things to happen) and new-world striving (newcomers to power who *make* things happen).

Of course, the Founders weren't perfect. They were men of their time. We daren't say another word before duly acknowledging the injustices of eighteenth-century society and the Founders' role in perpetuating them. Indentured servitude, debtors' prisons, women's subjugation, theft of Native American land, and African American slavery were all ills for which we could hold that generation accountable. But in comparison to the rest of the world at that time—the Barbary States, Qing China,

and Tsarist Russia spring to mind as alternatives—
America's founding gentlemen were as Enlightened
as it got.

While some colonials did seek to alter social
injustices outright, such as the early Quakers and
German pietists who protested slavery early in 1688,
many others dealt with inequity on a personal basis
in daily life. This latter group, when they had
influence as doctors, planters, lawyers, merchants,
and clergy affected change through micro acts of
daily benevolence. These are the people we might
think of as "ladies and gentlemen" in an American
sense (although that term would have been much
more strictly defined in eighteenth-century
England).

This American "gentry" saw the world through a
lens shaped by several ancient customs: Greco-
Roman philosophy, medieval chivalry, Renaissance
cultivation, and (most important) Judeo-Christian
religion. The Bible was the most popular book in
British North America by far, while Greek and Latin
also formed the backbone of a classical education.

A strong Greek influence was Plato's *Republic*, in
which he imagined an idealized city-state led by an
aristocracy of "guardians" trained to serve the
common good. These guardians would attend
special schools as children, serve in the military as
young men, rule the state in maturity, and serve as
counselors in old age. Their training would
emphasize courage, temperance, justice, arithmetic,

geometry, astronomy, music, and physical training. While learning to admire beauty and harmony, they would also be dangerous to enemies and generous with friends.

Plato's *Republic* was imaginary of course, but it set a mental standard for what benevolent leadership might look like. Roman influence was also strong. The American Founders admired the senatorial virtue of "gravitas" (dignity and seriousness) and they *really* liked Cincinnatus, the Roman statesman who (like Washington) left his farm to lead his country during a national emergency and then returned to the land after achieving victory.

There's a point to all this: If the United States of America is a nation founded by gentlemen, then on many deep levels our society must still operate on the assumption that people in power should demonstrate certain gentlemanly and ladylike attributes.

That is, we still expect people in authority to use their positions to help others as well as themselves. We don't expect powerful people in our country (whether they're elected officials or non-elected gatekeepers in finance, education, and media) to behave like Stalin, Mao Tse-tung, or even Huey Long. We pray for leaders to be more like Martin Luther King. We insist that every form of power should have *checks and balances* against every other form so no one can become a tyrant.

Indeed, whenever Americans get angry (or terrified) about where the country seems to be going, our concerns still revolve around an expectation of fairness and gentility amidst disagreement. As Robert Strausz-Hupé, founder of Philadelphia's Foreign Policy Research Institute, said in 1965: "Western democracy is gentlemanly representative government."[5]

We all Need Something to Shoot For

Anyway, as I said, all this stuff started occurring to me in late high school and early college. Of course, such thoughts didn't make for the best keg-party chatter. But if anyone had asked me back then what ultimate success in life would look like, I'd have said "I want to be the modern version of a garden-variety Founding Father—prosperous in business, civic minded, member of a militia, inventor of some new contraption, dabbler in art and literature, active in church, eager to roll up my sleeves to work the farm. All that with a lusty, ladylike wife to match." If most friends back then wanted to be grunge rock stars or lottery winners, this was my particular fantasy. Afterall, we all need something to shoot for.

---

[5] *In My Time: An Eclectic Autobiography* (New York: W.W. Norton, 1965).

Who Is a Gentleman?

Before we get on with the story about how I explored the gentlemanly ideal during my formative years, let's get some initial terms straight.

Specifically, who exactly qualifies as a gentleman? Traditionally, the answer to this question is misty. It's not at all easy to explain. In Shakespeare's time it described one with a right to bear arms who owned land. By the 19th century it became much more elastic. It always related to class but also transcended it, with no closed caste. It was both social and moral.

The recipe was based on many ingredients, but the final mix was (and still is) tough to spell out. A pinch of this, a dash of that. There's tremendous strength in this very vagueness; its ambiguity is what gives the idea its mystique and allure.

Non-Gentlemen: Delinquent Males

However, while it's hard to describe who is a gentleman, it's easier to describe his antithesis by using a delightful term coined by Derek Prince (more on him later): "delinquent males." *Delinquent males* are people with external genitalia who have no sense of duty toward others. For example, some of them treat sex as a sport, and once they get women into bed, may "ghost" their "conquests" afterward, ignoring their text messages. Of course, a spectrum from laddishness to caddishness exists, and what goes around comes around: guys who succumb to these temptations in youth often feel regret later in life if they're blessed with daughters. Delinquents may also cheat at sports, take the last nacho chip, and fail to pay debts. They fake a facade of decency when times are good. But when push comes to shove, they'd rather do the easy wrong thing instead of the difficult right thing.

Surely no one reading this has ever acted like a delinquent male, right? Sadly, if we're honest, we've all fallen short on occasion. For every man, it's a struggle (like weeding a garden) to keep one's inner delinquent in check. But by grace, we are all also works in progress.

Traditionally, in the Victorian lexicon, a delinquent male who behaved badly toward women was called a "cad." A fake gentleman was called a "bounder." If he was a real nasty piece of work, he'd be called a range of things like ruffian, thug, scoundrel, hooligan, villain, brute, or what have you.

While this covers some of the misanthropic aspects of being a non-gentleman, there are also some deceptively *nice-seeming* aspects that fall into delinquent male country because they involve abdicating one's responsibility to face conflict. Thus, a gentleman isn't just a "nice guy." He's not just a "people-pleaser" who says what he thinks people want to hear.

Men who are also Gentle

There once was a time when gentlemen came in four flavors: the sportsman, the soldier, the scholar, and the clergyman.[6] This implied a range of action and repose, extroversion and introspection. In each of these variations, a gentleman navigated various forms of *conflict* (physical, psychological, spiritual). As a result, he was likely to be both tactful and bluff. He was willing to laugh at affronts to himself but would defend a friend similarly attacked.

Knowing that he must respond to conflict in a gallant manner, he strengthened himself in advance however possible while also keeping a sense of *proportion*. If gentlemanliness were a compass, "proportion" would be one of its cardinal directions.

Today, as the cultural descendant of medieval knights, a gentleman is still a *warrior*—at war first and foremost with the delinquent male within himself. He guards against delinquent male urges whenever they want to act too aggressively or— which may be more common—too passively.

Back when I sat down to chip away at this definition, the *Wall Street Journal* posted an editorial by Peggy Noonan titled "America Needs More Gentlemen." It was an op-ed piece in response to the #MeToo movement following Hollywood producer Harvey Weinstein's sexual abuse scandals. After listing

---

[6] Philip Mason, The English Gentleman: The Rise and Fall of an Ideal (New York: William Morrow & Company, 1982).

various examples of delinquent-male behavior, Noonan said with exasperation, "I used to think America needed a parent to help it behave. Now I think it needs a grandparent." (Interesting how she puts the problem in generational terms.)

The article concluded: "In the past 40 years, in the movement for full equality, we [women] threw [the idea of the gentleman] over the side. But we should rescue that old and helpful way of being. The whole culture, especially women, needs The Gentleman back."[7]

Searching for a definition of gentlemanliness, Noonan said, "There are a million definitions of what a gentleman is, and some begin with references to being born to a particular standing," but she settled on an *Urban Dictionary* definition:

> "The true gentleman is the man whose conduct proceeds from good will . . . whose self-control is equal to all emergencies, who does not make the poor man conscious of his poverty, the obscure man of his obscurity, or any man of his inferiority or deformity."

Considering how obscene (albeit hilarious) some of *Urban Dictionary*'s bawdier definitions can be, their *gentleman* description is surprisingly accurate.

---

[7] Peggy Noonan, "America Needs More Gentlemen," *Wall Street Journal*, January 18, 2018, https://www.wsj.com/articles/america-needs-more-gentlemen-1516320167.

I would break things down to add that a gentleman is a *man* who is also *gentle*. This equation puts the *man* part first and the gentle part second. The "man" part is cake, so to speak, and the "gentle" part is icing.

If manhood is our starting point, then what on earth is a man? For most humans, our *fathers* set the crucial example of what it means to be a man. In some cases, these examples are splendid—in other cases tragic.

Three generations ago this question would have been much simpler to answer than it is today. Today, Facebook offers something like seventy-one (seventy-one!) gender options to describe what were once thought to be two—innie and outie. For some of us it's hard not to laugh at this degree of mind-boggling confusion. But for many, it's sensitive stuff, and a gentleman should respect everyone's opinion (up to a point).

Older Hollywood figures like Clint Eastwood, John Wayne, or Steve McQueen once stood as archetypes of masculinity. But of course, they were also caricatures invented by casting agents and screenwriters. For example, John Wayne, the gold standard for mid-century manhood, avoided the draft in World War II while pretending to be a marine on film, and instead of dressing like a gunslinger in daily life, he wore bespoke Brioni suits. Steve McQueen way have been more authentic off-screen, but even his sense of cool is hard to copy in real life.

Kipling's *If*

One of the cleanest manhood descriptions I've ever seen is spelled out in this poem by Rudyard Kipling called "If." It remains extremely popular in the United Kingdom today a century after its release:

If you can keep your head when all about you
Are losing theirs and blaming it on you,
If you can trust yourself when all men doubt you,
But make allowance for their doubting too;
If you can wait and not be tired by waiting,
Or being lied about, don't deal in lies,
Or being hated, don't give way to hating,
And yet don't look too good, nor talk too wise:

If you can dream —and not make dreams your master;
If you can think —and not make thoughts your aim;
If you can meet with Triumph and Disaster
And treat those two impostors just the same;
If you can bear to hear the truth you've spoken
Twisted by knaves to make a trap for fools,
Or watch the things you gave your life to, broken,
And stoop and build 'em up with worn-out tools:

If you can make one heap of all your winnings
And risk it on one turn of pitch-and-toss,
And lose, and start again at your beginnings
And never breathe a word about your loss;
If you can force your heart and nerve and sinew
To serve your turn long after they are gone,

And so hold on when there is nothing in you
Except the Will which says to them: "Hold on!"

If you can talk with crowds and keep your virtue,
Or walk with Kings—nor lose the common touch,
If neither foes nor loving friends can hurt you,
If all men count with you, but none too much;
If you can fill the unforgiving minute
With sixty seconds' worth of distance run,
Yours is the Earth and everything that's in it,
And—which is more—you'll be a Man, my son![8]

Now, if you're anything like me, you probably just skimmed through Kipling's poem above without really reading it. At any rate, that's what I normally do whenever an author quotes verse.

But this poem is *important*, so let's consider it again in colloquial speech. Here's how I would rephrase Kipling if you were to ask me to describe it while sitting in traffic on our way to the airport:

> "Stay calm when others are freaking out and saying it's all your fault. Trust yourself when others think you're crazy, but also double-check to see if they have a point.

> "Learn to be patient, even when it sucks, because good things (like oak trees) often take time to develop.

---

[8] Rudyard Kipling, "If," 1910, accessed on Wikipedia, https://en.wikipedia.org/wiki/If%E2%80%94.

"If others lie about you, don't lie about them in return. If others hate you, don't hate them back. Try to be the best you can be at all times, but don't try to look too good while doing it (because that will trigger envy).

"Dream big and think great thoughts, but don't spend so much time dreaming about something that you can't bring it to reality.

"Triumph and Disaster are both 'impostors.' They don't really exist. When you think you're on top of the world, things aren't really all that perfect; and when you feel like a total failure, things aren't perfectly bad.

"And when you put all you've got into something and it falls apart, let yourself cry about it for a while (preferably in private), but consider getting back in there to rebuild from scratch.

"Get yourself as physically fit as possible so you don't have to be a weak link in times of crisis when you should have the chance to shine.

"Be socially flexible, like the cool guy in school who could sit equally comfortably at the most popular lunch table or with the most painfully awkward people while also having his own normal friends.

27

"People make mistakes all the time, especially those whom you love best.

"Admittedly, this is a long laundry list of stuff to have in your character, but if you can manage pulling it together even somewhat over the long haul, you'll be a hero."

Kipling suggests that manliness requires constant cultivation of personal strength (intellectual, emotional, physical, social) and resilience to adversity. Such a focus might be criticized today as a form of "toxic masculinity." Surely, Kipling's poem could apply equally well to lionhearted women as well as men. In either case, these traits make up what have traditionally been called "the manly virtues." (I've seen Victorian/ Edwardian writers describe English *women* as "manly," and they meant it as a compliment.)

The Forbearing Use of Power

Many effective leaders in history have been able to blend Kipling's tough, stoic form of character with equally strong amounts of sensitivity and empathy. It implies the ability to give orders and see that they're obeyed while doing this without force and with enough consideration to avoid resentment.

Robert E. Lee famously described a gentleman as one who manages power in nuanced, tender ways. A decent man in a terrible moral situation if there ever was one, Lee wrestled with how to wield the "forbearing use of power." His famous definition is worth quoting in full:

> The forbearing use of power does not only form a touchstone, but the manner in which an individual enjoys certain advantages over others is a test of a true gentleman.
>
> The power which the strong have over the weak, the employer over the employed, the educated over the unlettered, the experienced over the confiding, even the clever over the silly—the forbearing or inoffensive use of all this power or authority, or a total abstinence from it when the case admits it, will show the gentleman in a plain light.
>
> The gentleman does not needlessly and unnecessarily remind an offender of a wrong he may have committed against him. He cannot only forgive, he can forget; and he strives for that nobleness of self and mildness of character which impart sufficient strength to let the past be but the past. A true man of honor feels humbled himself when he cannot help humbling others.[9]

[9] "Definition of a Gentleman," University of Virginia, accessed February 1, 2019, http://xroads.virginia.edu/~CAP/LEE/gentdef.html;

We could update and extend Lee's definition by saying that *anyone* who has *any* advantage over others is in the position to be a lady (gentlewoman) or gentleman *if* they exercise that authority with lovingkindness. Thus, if you're a good athlete in gym class, you're more "empowered" (to use a social-justice term) than the kids who can't throw and catch (like me as a kid, alas). If you're a stressed-out mom with toddlers, you wield tremendous power over their human destinies. The point here is that subtle matters of status permeate all human relationships constantly.

Each of us has advantages and disadvantages in every interaction. A lady or gentleman seeks to be *aware* of such fleeting hierarchies in order to smooth them over however possible, to level the playing field by personal example. Every day, each of us has the option to be genteel or thuggish as we navigate such things.

"Lee, Southern Gentleman," University of Virginia, accessed February 1, 2019, http://xroads.virginia.edu/~CAP/LEE/lee2.html.

The Dutch Bombshell

Speaking of personal authority reminds me of a girl I met in college who changed my life without intending to.

As I mentioned earlier, when I was a kid, I couldn't have cared less about gentility, or manners, or duty to others. This started to change however through a series of romantic episodes in college that revealed my rough edges quite uncomfortably. Human nature being what it is, I often learned the most not when things were going well, but whenever disappointments came my way. The biggest of these experiences began senior year, when a gorgeous Dutch exchange student appeared on campus.

She was six feet tall with copious blond hair and blueberry eyes which seemed to flash beams of light when she smiled. She could easily have been a model or supermodel, and she caught me so off guard the night we first met in a muggy August crowded room that I had to dart outside for air.

But to call her a "bombshell" is to tell merely half the story. She was also kind and warm-hearted in a friendly girl-next-door kind of way. And she was a touch naive. Upon meeting her my Mom said, "she's just like the farmer's daughter." Other guys might not have seen the total package I saw that night, but it was enough to make me swoon with "shell shock."

For weeks after that first encounter, I wandered around campus like Young Werther dreaming about how to make a move. I finally struck upon the idea of inviting her on a bike ride in Lancaster County. (Somehow, I knew that Dutch people like bicycles.) So, I asked her. And she said "Yes." I borrowed my roommate's bike for her, raised the seat as far up as it could go to accommodate her astounding length, and watched with no small interest as she swung a leg over the frame and rested her hips on the saddle. A nod between us, and we were off.

As we pedaled along, my initial nervousness evaporated with effortless small talk. The more we rode, the more we bridged whatever distance lay between us from having grown up on separate continents. As the miles clicked away that warm sunny day, it dawned on me that Gisela (not her real name) wasn't just a gorgeous exchange student— she might well be my future wife!

The reason I mention this with such detail is that when a twenty-one-year-old knucklehead starts thinking about marrying a girl he just met, his whole universe changes. He finds himself suddenly wanting to be a *better man*. He finds himself wanting to please her and change in ways he might have thought ludicrous when his mom originally trained him back home. Habits and characteristics his parents spent years (unsuccessfully) trying to get him to amend will vanish in a heartbeat if he thinks his new crush won't approve of them.

Anyway, that's how it was for me with Gisela. And that's how I've seen it with countless other guys when they first fall hard. "Toxic masculinity" rants notwithstanding, when guys fall, they often fall *hard*. Had Gisela grown up in a cave, I would have wanted to become a caveman. Had she grown up in the circus, I would have wanted to be an acrobat. But as it turned out, she came from a somewhat aristocratic ("haute bourgeois" to be more accurate) family with strong rules of lifestyle and etiquette.

As we got to know each other, Gisela revealed that her brother and sister belonged to an elite student fraternity where new kids got slapped in the face if they made mistakes at the dinner table. "They have to know the etiquettes," she memorably said. Much to my benefit, Gisela took this knowledge and attempted to civilize me as an American regarding such things. To my immense happiness, she adopted me as her "best friend" that year. But to my excruciation, her affection went no further. In such situations can anything be worse than the dreaded "friend zone?" As anyone knows who has experienced unrequited love in any one of its many terrible forms, words can't do justice. It's like passing an emotional kidney stone daily. The less said about it the better.

But friend zone or not, she made such a good impact on me, I'm glad to have suffered. For it was she who first got me thinking about the importance of being a gentleman in modern terms. Of course, her background was purely providential. Had Gisela been a cowgirl, I'd have harnessed my efforts into roping steers.

And she didn't just teach me through personal example in America. That would never have done the trick. What really put the hook in my gill was when I got to see how she lived back at her home in Holland. That's what really catapulted the journey.

When she went home for Christmas that winter, a buddy and I happened to be doing a much-awaited rail trip in Europe. Knowing we'd be in the neighborhood, she invited us to a "shooting day" at a country house with a mote around it (no joke), where people shot rabbits and pheasants in driven hunts. We arrived just in time to see gamekeepers blowing trumpets over dead rodents lined up on the ground while others stood around in Barbour jackets and Wellington boots looking like extras in a Ralph Lauren ad. Indeed, had I seen them in an actual Polo ad, I'd have dismissed it as over the top. But there it was plain and simple, and the whole image struck me. The neatest thing was how well they blended English country living, with French good living, and Dutch warm-heartedness. It set a standard that has influenced me ever since.

Through exposure to such things in Holland, and during many other times together in America, Gisela taught me a lot. Of course, I also taught her things as well that she'd have never picked up otherwise. In this sense we were truly "exchange students"

Acting is Interacting

When Gisela returned to Pennsylvania for spring semester, she and I enrolled in an acting class for an art credit that surprisingly taught each of us things that made us a better lady and gentleman. Not in the mannerly sense of being right and proper, but more in the sense of tailoring your behavior to interact with people on a "theatrical" level. (Of course, leadership and acting are quite related. There's an old saying that a woman once asked World War II general Dwight Eisenhower if he knew Douglas MacArthur, to which Ike replied, "Yes, I studied drama under General MacArthur for four years in the Philippines.")

Our instructor, who insisted we call her by her first name Pam, knew all about "method acting" from studying under Sanford Meisner in New York City. Her classes were like group therapy sessions. We practiced something called Alba Emoting, where you learned how to bring emotions to the surface by making faces representing them. That is, you'd make a face on the surface hoping the emotion would follow underneath, and sometimes it did. This taught me a reverse lesson that you could also refuse to make a face, and by refusing, you could keep unwanted emotions at bay.

We also performed improvisational skits, monologues, and exercises where you had to sit on the floor across from someone and guess their inner thoughts based on the faces they made. It was dashed awkward if you didn't like the other person, but quite fun if you did. Gisela and I later played this game for laughs outside of class with hilarious results.

The aim of all this was for each "actor" to get outside him or herself and inside other people. It was a way of training *empathy*, which is a crucial skill for leadership and an antidote to genuine toxic masculinity.

Our acting lessons also emphasized forming *ensemble* among actors as a team. The main idea here was to focus your attention on *others* instead of yourself. "Acting is *interacting*," Pam would say over and over until it became a mantra, "Acting is *interacting*."

Pam stressed that actors are only compelling when they are *generous*—when their energy flows *outward*. She said that if you go on stage with a neediness for the audience to love you, they'll probably find you repellent because they'll react to your selfishness without even knowing it. By contrast, if you walk on stage with "generous" energy, focusing on your fellow actors and on the events occurring in the plot, the audience would find you compelling. Gisela and I both saw how these ideas didn't just apply to acting but to life in general.

The month before it was time for Gisela to return to Holland, we took a road trip through New England, seeing new sights, talking seamlessly, and singing to songs she had on a mix tape, such as things from Cat Stevens' or Simon and Garfunkel. There was such an innocence about it. It was like being nine years old again, but with a driver's license. We'd share long silences that would eventually break when one said, "What are you thinking right this very moment?" Being friend-zoned with her was still excruciating—especially when we shared hotel rooms on that trip—but it showed me how nice things could be when you find someone with whom you connect.

A few weeks later when I drove her to the airport for her return flight home, it seemed impossible that this could be the end. At the last minute, I turned to her in the car, hoping for a Hallmark Special turn-around and said, "Are you *sure* you never had a crush on me romantically during all the time we spent together this past year?" But she looked at me blankly and, with Dutch candor said, "No." A Victorian gentleman may have been the sort of chap who never cried, but not this American. For a week or so after Gisela left the country, I went for long drives through Lancaster County to let it all out. Once that gusher ran its course, the bleeding heart stopped, and the wound cauterized.

But there were such benefits from those times with Gisela. By the time her year in America ended, she and I were much more developed personalities than we were before we met. The experience taught me that a guy can really develop when the right woman comes along to influence him. Putting on my historian cap, I can now say I unwittingly followed the path of the medieval troubadours who found themselves wanting to be better knights when they fell in love with unattainable ladies.

Gisela changed my life's trajectory primarily because of the ways in which she was my *superior*. She matched me at every point, and by many metrics she surpassed me. My dad even said as much. In retrospect, it was great to meet someone who challenged me that way. A few years before that, as a high-school senior I was pretty accomplished: swimming team captain, Eagle Scout, Winter Ball King, leading role in the school musical (*Brigadoon*). According to my sister, girls had crushes on me, and I never knew it.

But then Gisela came along and trumped all that. Scripture says that God opposes the proud and gives grace to the humble. If that is true, he couldn't have invented a better vessel to humble me.

As time passed, the Gisela episode continued paying dividends. She stayed in my memory like a burr in the saddle, like an electric cattle prod for personal development. She put sand in my oyster that later became pearls. Is there a lesson here for young men wanting to become better gentlemen? Yes! Seek bright, strong, accomplished, refined women (i.e. ladies) who challenge you to be your best self. Don't squander yourself with easy layups. As iron sharpens iron, strong people sharpen each other.

Leveling Upward

Although I was initially much too preoccupied with Gisela romantically to think about her as a learning experience (that would come later), she managed to do something for me that University of Pennsylvania sociologist Digby Baltzell described as "leveling upward."[10]

Leveling *upward* is a way to aim for human equality by holding everyone to high standards. It's the opposite of "leveling *downward*," which attempts to achieve equality by lowering everyone's standards to the lowest common denominator. Both approaches attempt to solve a conundrum implied in the Declaration of Independence:

- All men (humans) are created equal, but
- All human talents are not distributed equally.

We've each inherited different talents, flaws, and blessings. Social scientists may act as if they understand what causes such discrepancies, but the truth is probably a mystery that won't be solved this side of eternity. Leveling upward assumes that by becoming the best person you can possibly be, and treating others better than yourself, you can improve the lives of everyone around you.

---

[10] Digby Baltzell, *Sporting Gentlemen: Men's Tennis from the Age of Honor to the Cult of the Superstar*, 1st ed. (New York: Free Press, 1995).

Graduate School at Durham, England

After Gisela left for Holland, I started wondering why we had so much in common despite having grown up on opposite sides of the Atlantic.

Protestant Cultural Roots

That year, by coincidence (or providence) I discovered some books by E. Digby Baltzell, who studied what was once called the "protestant establishment," i.e. the people who set America's tone of thought during the country's first three centuries.

When I read *Puritan Boston and Quaker Philadelphia*, his dense study about the impact of religion on those two cities, I realized that Gisela's culture in the Netherlands was influenced by Calvinism, just as my Protestant heritage was influenced by it the United States. That is, we both came from cultures that had once been deeply influenced by "bourgeois values" and Reformed theology. We were thus members of an intellectual "tribe" without even knowing it. This got me thinking about how families pass their values down through generations even as the main-stream societies around them change.

To explore these cultural roots deeper, I got the idea that living in a formerly Calvinist country such England, Scotland, Switzerland, Germany, or the Netherlands might reveal things about my own inherited assumptions that lay hidden. Of all these options, England, with its direct link to Old Philadelphia, seemed like the best place to start. In retrospect I laugh at this train of thought because there's nothing more American than going to an "old country" to explore one's roots. I recently spoke to an acquaintance who did the same thing in Liberia.

Through friendly recommendations, I discovered the University of Durham, a place in northern England which seemed like a combination of Duke University and Trinity College in America—decent academic institutions with a preppy twist. The guy who mentioned Durham said it with raised eyebrows, as if it were a big deal. Finding an undiscovered "big deal" is always exciting. And to make the proposition even better, Durham was an extremely *pragmatic* option. It cost much less money to get a master's degree in the UK than it would in the US, it took *half* the time, and you didn't have to fuss with GREs.

That summer I took a trip to spy out the land.

The best way to see Durham for the first time is to sit on the right-hand side of the train heading north from London to Edinburgh. As you approach the city, the train goes through a wooded area for a while, it rounds a bend, and then *boom*, a magnificent Norman cathedral and castle burst into view. You hop off and start descending lots of steps from the viaduct to reach the town below.

Clomping through town on foot (it always felt like "clomping" because of the cobblestones), I explored the place at whim, working up a sweat by jogging the narrow stone closes (alley ways), getting intentionally lost in the disorienting medieval streets, ducking into shops for coffees and eats, balancing on stone walls, and sitting at pubs in the evening to chat with anyone in earshot over a pint.

The weather that day was overcast, with heavy clouds rolling overhead blocking the sun for long minutes at a time, and then opening up again to brilliant blue sky for equally long spells. The contrast between brightness and darkness warned me that Durham might be pleasant or depressing depending on the weather. But happy or sad, the town was *gorgeous*—it won me over. In a sense, my attraction to Durham was just as automatic as my affection for Gisela the year before. Just as I knew on the Lancaster county bike ride that I'd marry her if she'd have me, I knew within a day that I couldn't not attend Durham *if* they would have me.

For Americans, the British university structure can seem confusing. Like Oxford and Cambridge, Durham University was composed of *colleges*—tiny communities where students lived. Each of these had its own character. Among the oldest "bailey colleges" were University, Hatfield, and St. Chad's. I picked St. Chad's College because, having come from a small town (coincidently called Collegeville) it was the smallest.

After applying and waiting for months that seemed like years, Chad's sent an acceptance letter in 1999 inviting me to matriculate in 2000. My master's program would be "taught," which meant that I would work one-on-one with a tutor. The tutorial method is a tremendous way to learn.

When I arrived at Durham, our history department chairman gave a speech that first week in which he joked, "We still take an amateur approach to historical studies in Britain. It's as if history were something gentlemen do in their spare time between playing cricket and defending the empire." He said this totally whimsically of course, but I took it absolutely seriously, convinced that most of the world's problems could be solved with a resurrection of the gentlemanly ideal. His offhand comment further primed me for studying about the underpinnings of this concept in earnest.

Later that week, my adviser invited me to his office to discuss what I wanted to study the coming year. I had to pinch myself. After years of going to school and sitting through classes I cared nothing about, it was amazing to have the freedom to study whatever the heck I wanted, and to set my own program. The English system had a genius for such flexibility.

Glancing around his office packed to the gills with overflowing bookcases (each of which he'd presumably read), I told him I wanted to learn about how the idea of the British gentleman developed during the century between 1850 to 1950. That timeframe nicely bookended the mid-nineteenth and early twentieth centuries through both World Wars—a time which saw the peak of the British Empire and its global transition to Pax Americana. During that century, British mores greatly influenced the American political, business, and social establishment. I figured that by learning about British views during that era, I could learn something about American to boot.

The next week my advisor gave me a multi-page list of books to read over the coming year, covering a range of topics related to my subject. Each week he would assign me a few of these books, I'd read them, and we would discuss them in person. This one-on-one built tremendous endurance for plowing through volumes as I would have never attempted to do back home. It was a great way to learn, with nowhere to hide.

British Public Schools

Any meditation on gentlemanliness would require that I first learn about the British public schools, because these organizations formed a nucleus of the idea for generations. As institutions designed for training an aristocracy in the "habit of command," they were intentionally elitist. They took for granted many of the class dynamics Americans may be familiar with from watching the TV series *Downton Abbey*.

At the time when *Downton Abbey's* first episode began (1912) there were nine major public schools in Britain and nearly three hundred others, each with its own niche. To clarify for American readers, these British schools were "public" in the sense that students lived there full-time in surrogate families away from home. But they were privately funded, and therefore not public in the American sense of general admission state-funded high schools. In other words, they were like American "prep" schools.

Although the oldest of these schools date back centuries, they assumed special importance during the Industrial Revolution when newly rich businessmen amassed more wealth than the landed aristocracy and gentry. Feeling threatened by the new kids on the block, the landed classes managed a clever switcheroo. They got businesspeople to send their sons to these drafty old public schools, where boys were trained to think and act like landed gentlemen. By extension, they also learned to despise the mercantile values of their fathers.

A social blending occurred in which middle class boys acquired aristocratic values such as chivalry, panache, aplomb... (in a word, "tone") while aristocrats acquired the more bourgeois virtues of industry, moderation, thrift... (in a word, "reliability"). Digby Baltzell said, "In the segregated democracy of the boarding school, sons of the nobility, the gentry, and the rising middle classes could be molded into one gentlemanly class."[11]

Spoiled Rich Kids

In the 1830s, Rugby School was a thought-leader in this evolution. Its headmaster Thomas Arnold was a devout Christian who reformed the school on evangelical lines. He distrusted both the reactionary Toryism of the landed classes and the crude materialism of the new industrial rich, and he believed the upper classes had been failing to do their duty to the poor. To remedy this, "he aimed to produce a class of educated, truth-telling, Christian gentlemen who would stand aloof from both the new materialism and the old ossifying Toryism."[12] In a sense, he also wanted to mold spoiled rich kids into benevolent "guardians," as Plato envisioned in *The Republic*. With time, his methods influenced similar schools around the world.

Arnold's hierarchy of values was the exact opposite of our schools today:

- Morals came first;
- Sportsmanship came second; and
- Intellectual achievement came third.

---

[11] Digby Baltzell, *Sporting Gentlemen: Men's Tennis from the Age of Honor to the Cult of the Superstar*, 1st ed. (New York: Free Press, 1995).
[12] Ibid.

It might seem obvious that Arnold the evangelist would place morals first, but why did he rank *sportsmanship* above academic scholarship? Because he saw team sports like rowing, rugby, and cricket as vehicles for building valuable character traits such as loyalty, self-sacrifice, and endurance.

He and headmasters at other schools assumed that rich kids would be worthless citizens in adult life if they were self-centered and spoiled, so they aimed to toughen boys up by making school life intentionally *harsh*. Believing that civilizations rose on hardihood and collapsed with luxury and effeminacy, they hoped to avoid a repeat of the 1789 French Revolution by making each new British generation "more simple, more hardy, more Christian than the last."[13] To this end, the richest, most elite schools in the world were uncomfortable, ill-equipped, and slightly medieval.

Rooms were frigid in winter. Boys performed outdoor sports in all weather and had to bathe in cold water. Hot-water baths were blamed for bringing down the Roman Empire. Reminiscing about his years at Marlborough College, one man recalled, "Throughout winter's rages, the windows of the dormitories were always kept wide open so that one sometimes woke up to find that one was sleeping under a coverlet of snow... We were always cold."

---

[13] Philip Mason, The English Gentleman: The Rise and Fall of an Ideal (New York: William Morrow & Company, 1982).

Boys were also trained through *food*. They were given one meal per day with additional "commons" (scraps of bread and cheese) at other times. If boys wanted anything else to eat, they had to buy it and cook it themselves. "It was good for character to learn that if all your pocket money was spent by half term, there would be no more jam or eggs or sausages before the holidays." [14]

In direct contrast to twenty-first-century mores, many Victorian educators turned a blind eye to bullying, which they also considered a tool for character development. Instead of running to adults for aid, boys were encouraged to stand up for themselves and even gang up against tormentors. Such policy was hardly Christian. And in a sense, there was a spiritual battle going on between charitable Christian discipline and a harsher materialist, scientific-racist, neo-Spartan, social Darwinist view of people like Herbert Spencer which dismissed Christian charity as an excuse for collective weakness.[15]

In some ways, Victorian public-schools were a tribal indoctrination process like modern Marine Corps boot camp. Life was a choreographed struggle against privation, adversity, and callousness in various forms. And like boot camp—or an iron foundry's annealing process—it began with intense

---

[14] Ibid.
[15] J.A. Mangan, Manliness and Morality: Middle-Class Masculinity in Britain and America, 1800-1940 (London: St. Martin's Press, 1978).

heat that was painful at first but gradually eased up each year.

Youngsters learned their place in a graded society governed by unwritten rules created by prior generations of boys. A rule created spur of the moment in jest one year might become rigid custom ("we've always done it this way") a decade later. Many of these were tree-fort childish, but no less compelling. A first-year kid might be forbidden from putting his hands in his pockets or carrying a furled umbrella. As he progressed each year, he would gain such privileges incrementally, taking extra care to ensure that his own underclassmen didn't overstep the very bounds he once obeyed. Eventually, through a system called "fagging" ("fag" is a nineteenth-century boarding school term that originally had nothing to do with sexuality), the boy who once cleaned boots and buttered bread for his superiors would have younger boys doing similar tasks for him.

It was hoped that by experiencing these extremes of servitude and command, a young gentleman would enter adult life with equal measures of compassion and confidence.

The Prefect System: "Boy Rule"

Convinced that boys would better develop morally if taught by example, Arnold introduced a *prefect system*, which allowed exemplary senior boys to run their boarding houses. "It was one of the secrets of his achievement that, in spite of his deep sense of the wickedness of the world in general, and of boys in particular," that Arnold delegated such power."[16] Often called "boy rule," the system was taken quite seriously. Holding court in the house "library," head boys would assign daily chores to keep the building shipshape. Their local government would legislate, judge offenses, and punish offenders with liberal use of the cane. Corporal punishment was deemed essential among people who later expected the same ruthless pursuit of excellence in the army or navy.

To modern sensibilities, the Victorian prefect system is astonishing. At Marlboro, prefects acquired such responsibility that when one of them ran to his adult housemaster telling him their building was on fire, the housemaster waved him off saying, "That part of the house is your department, not mine!"[17]

Trained for Crisis

Nineteenth-century public schools could certainly be brutal. Social Darwinism took the character thing way too far, and some boys were emotionally crippled for life. There's a saying that public schools produced men with well "well-trained bodies, half-trained minds, and undeveloped hearts." But the

---

[16] Philip Mason, The English Gentleman: The Rise and Fall of an Ideal (New York: William Morrow & Company, 1982).

[17] J.A. Mangan, Manliness and Morality: Middle-Class Masculinity in Britain and America, 1800-1940 (London: St. Martin's Press, 1978).

system also produced men with tremendous grit. As British prime minister Stanley Baldwin said,

> "The Englishman is made for a time of crisis, and for a time of emergency. He is serene in difficulties but may seem to be indifferent when times are easy. He may not look ahead, he may not heed warnings, he may not prepare, but once he starts, he is persistent to the death and he is ruthless in action."[18]

All this was illustrated by a saying, "An Englishman loses every battle, but the last."

Describing life at such a school in the 1960s, Christopher Hitchens said, "True, I did get pushed around and unfairly punished and introduced too soon to some distressing facts of existence, but I would not have preferred to stay at home or to have been sheltered from these experiences." And, "one may in fact be very slightly better equipped to face that Japanese jail or Iraqi checkpoint."[19]

As the British Empire reached its apogee, its public-school system attracted attention globally. Its blending of middle-class morality and aristocratic chivalry created a standard for gentlemanly

---

[18] Philip Mason, The English Gentleman: The Rise and Fall of an Ideal (New York: William Morrow & Company, 1982).
[19] Christopher Hitchens, Hitch 22 a Memoir (New York: Hachette Book Group, 2010).

behavior respected the world over.[20] The system even infused gallantry into commercial life.

For example, when the San Francisco earthquake struck in 1906, causing stupendous losses for insurance companies in both the US and UK, greedy American firms quickly hired lawyers to seek ways to avoid paying their rightful claims. By contrast, Lloyds of London underwriter Cuthbert Heath, trained as a gentleman, did the exact opposite. He ordered his San Francisco agent to fully pay all policyholders regardless of their policy terms.[21]

Heath's gesture assumes heroic meaning if you consider that he was on the hook with *unlimited liability* for all these claims. Had demands exceeded cash reserves, he would have had to cover the difference with all his personal property "down to his brace buttons" (a custom jokingly referred to as "financial Hara-kiri"). His action solidified Lloyd's reputation in the United States for years to come. And it all stemmed from a gentlemanly honor code that held money (and one's own personal comfort and safety) in slight contempt.

---

[20] *In My Time: An Eclectic Autobiography* (New York: W.W. Norton, 1965).
[21] "San Francisco Earthquake," Lloyd's, accessed December 28, 2018, https://www.lloyds.com/about-lloyds/history/catastrophes-and-claims/san-francisco-1906-earthquake.

Spoiled Rich Kids No More

As I read all these books about British public-school mores, among the most memorable was Paul Fussell's *The Great War and Modern Memory*[22] in which he described fascinating things about the British penchant for *improvisation* (doing things ad hoc and on the fly). He described how rich young men, accustomed to luxury at home, spent months in squalid, rat-infested trenches taking care of their men while trying to be cheerful. He made a big deal of a thing called "British phlegm," in which one tried to understate things with short, pithy comments—a style that Ernest Hemingway later copied in his novels.

In short, Fussell described a style of reserved masculinity that appealed to me greatly: confident enough to be effete on the outside but tough as nails inside. An iron fist in a velvet glove.

Public Schools' Influence in America

As I read about the British schools, I also learned how they impacted elite education in America. The most famous instance was Groton, a Massachusetts school founded by Endicott Peabody in 1884. Inspired by Arnold's servant-leadership ideal, Peabody adopted the motto *cui servire est regnare*, "To serve is to reign."

---

[22] Paul Fussell, *The Great War and Modern Memory* (USA: Oxford University Press, 1975).

Groton struck the fancy of America's industrial aristocracy just as it was forming. Peabody created scarcity value by limiting the school's enrollment and as its popularity spread. This triggered expansion through cell division as similar Episcopal church schools sprung up on his model. Today the earliest of these are known as "St. Grotlesex" (St. Marks, St. Paul's, St. George's, Groton, and Middlesex).

The Episcopalian view of servant-leadership assumed a sense of "nobles oblige" (*to whom much is given, much is required*) that emphasized a "life of service and of heroism, preferably in war but if necessary, in one of its moral equivalents."[23]

Like the American Founders, Peabody didn't merely ape old-world views. he blended them with new-world dynamism. "Groton became more fevered, more messianic, more of a City on a Hill than Rugby, Eton, or Harrow would ever be. The English schools were too civilized in a worldly way, too old-world aristocratic. Peabody wanted to create a moral aristocracy in the tradition of his Puritan ancestors, who considered themselves the pioneers of New England, vastly superior to the decadent citizens of Old England."[24] With such feelings an American once visited Eton and said, "Ah, the Groton of England, I believe?"

---

[23] Ibid.

[24] Kit Konolige, *The Power of Their Glory* (New York: Simon and Schuster, 1978).

Gentlemanly Character and the Boy Scouts

By the twentieth century, British public-school values had fans the world over. With an urge to "level-upward," there was an honest effort to teach upper class mores to working class boys. It might be a stretch to call such an effort "democratic" but it was inclusive, after a fashion. Lord Robert Baden-Powell founded the Boy Scout movement, "as an education in the code for youth unfortunate enough not to be trained at Eton."[25] Indeed, the Scout Oath and Scout Law are honor codes rooted in both the "bourgeois values" and medieval chivalry:

> *On my honor, I will do my best to do my duty to God and my country, and to obey the Scout Law, to keep myself physically strong, mentally awake, and morally straight.*

A Scout is: *Trustworthy*
                       Loyal
                       Helpful
                       Friendly
                       Courteous
                       Kind
                       Obedient
                       Cheerful
                       Thrifty
                       Brave
                       Clean
                       Reverent

---

[25] Nathaniel Burt, *The Perennial Philadelphians: The Anatomy of an American Aristocracy* (Boston: Little, Brown, 1963).

As a young boy, I was probably exposed to "British" gentlemanly views through the Boy Scouts of America before anywhere else. Its combined emphasis on adventure and service appealed to me implicitly as a little boy reading my dad's Scout handbook from the 1950s. Perhaps, on some level, Baden-Powell's efforts to form young gentlemen in nations beyond the Empire helped influence my journey to Durham. It certainly built a respect for living outdoors, roughing it, and seeking wild situations while remaining tidy and clean-cut yourself.

British versus American Pride

One thing that immediately struck me in Durham was how *well* everyone spoke. Many of the English students there seemed oh so eloquent—even the ones who weren't all that bright. And for a country so small, it surprised me how many people seemed to speak with different accents. Each region had its own idiosyncrasy and seemed to produce its own style of speech. People generally seemed to have broader vocabularies, and they played with their words much more than we Americans do. For lack of a better word, their speech seemed *baroque*, with curlicues and flourishes you wouldn't hear in Anywhere USA.

Also, more importantly—and much more fun—they were always ready for *humor*. You had to assume that anything anyone said at any given time might have been meant as a joke. Often, I'd often get caught off guard by such quips and find myself laughing loudly. During daily after-lunch bull sessions with Martin, Dave, Ben, and Tom up in Kevin's room the banter was lightning quick, evoking genuine belly laughs even to the point of rolling around on the floor.

This readiness for laughter taught me something about being a gentleman that I could never have learned in the United States: Britons seemed to make a point of *never getting offended*. For example, when Americans say, "That offends me," they act as if getting offended were something to be proud of. As if, linked to their "self-esteem," it makes them de facto "special" just for registering an affront. In England it was the opposite. To allow yourself to get offended was to demonstrate weakness. Any self-respecting Brit prefers to give the impression that he or she is simply above caring.

Apparently, this attitude goes way back. In the 1830s, Alexis de Tocqueville observed, "an Englishman will quietly enjoy whatever real or imagined advantages he believes himself to possess, while an American will tell everyone about them . . . The Englishman grants nothing to anyone, nor does he ask for any confirmation in return . . . His pride needs no nourishment; it feeds on itself."[26]

A few years ago, I heard a man sum it up this way: "Americans want to tell you how great they are. Britishers expect you to know how great they are without being told." This distinction is very, very interesting. Although pride is a vice that brings much more trouble than it's worth, the understated English way of managing it certainly demonstrates more self-confidence.

The approach to sportsmanship revealed another major difference between Britain and America. At Durham sports were a *big deal*, just as they are in American schools and universities. But the British approach to winning and losing was much different from ours. We Americans place *winning* above all

---

[26] Alexis de Tocqueville, *Democracy in America* (New York: Library of America, 2004).

else, while the British care more about how you play the game. If we wink at competitors who skirt the rules when the referee isn't looking, the British take pride in toeing the line. Such discipline, which is a form of bravery, often comes at great personal cost. For them, *HOW* you win is more important than *IF* you win. It's a legacy of Thomas Arnold's public-school tradition. Losing gallantly is a way to show panache, and it's yet another way to demonstrate that you're simply above caring.

St. Chad's College Boat Club

Dialing into this ethos, I was eager to take up a sport. I attempted rugby for a week but decided to quit when huge team mate laid a bear-sized paw on my shoulder and said, "Mate, you may be small and thin, but you're probably quick and nimble, right?" "No . . ." I said. "I'm small *and* slow."

So, I switched to rowing with the St. Chad's College Boat Club. This was much a better fit, as rowing required simple bodily movements and dogged endurance. After an embarrassing learning curve "catching crabs" and nearly capsizing, I won a spot on the "College Eight" (their main boat). This feat would have been impossible for me at any college other than Durham's smallest. Twenty years on, my rowing singlet with "SCCBC" and crossed oars emblazoned on the chest lies neatly stowed in a foot locker should I ever need it again.

Oddly, I discovered it was easier to learn rowing techniques by writing notes about them on paper than it was to just pay attention by ear. This made me realize that some people literally learn through their pens. For example, if the coach said, "do this and don't do that," her instruction wouldn't really register until I sat down afterward and "locked it in" by writing describing it in a notebook.

At Durham we held frequent rowing regattas, and these were often *gorgeous*. Lavish with British pageantry (as I saw it), with everything in its place, lots of color and organized chaos. On frosty mornings hundreds of boats would back up in traffic jams on the River Wear, coxswains bellowing, oarsmen smacking blades with passing boats, experts sweeping along in a preening fashion, novices looking shaky and occasionally swamping.

Gliding under bridges on the narrow river, it was marvelous to feel the occasional "clunk" when our blades caught the water in perfect unison. Healthwise, it was a full-body workout: upper, lower, and midsection engaging each stroke in a one-rep max. It was absolutely team oriented, with no chance whatsoever for individual displays of prowess. The best oarsman is he who blends in. Having always done individual sports back in high school, this chance to anonymously blend into a crew was lifechanging.

The training schedule was delightfully hit-and-miss. We'd wake up at 5:00 AM never knowing until the last minute if the river was calm enough for rowing. If the current was too fast, or if the boathouse was flooded from rain, we'd get the luxury of tucking in to a massive "full cooked" breakfast of bacon, eggs, sausage, baked beans, stewed tomatoes, orange juice, coffee, and toast.

But training had a sinister side: the ergometer (rowing machine). Each week we had to do an all-out 5-kilometer pull to remain on the college Eight. On the "ergo" (as they called it) or "erg" as we call it in America, there was no-place to hide. With the coach watching your splits and screaming into your ear, it was a weekly torture session in lactic acid. Years later when I was in the military, there were rarely any situations that surpassed the misery of "erging" at Durham.

Civilized Barbarity

On Sundays I attended Anglican mass at either St. Chad's chapel or Durham Cathedral, which was right across the street. Anglicanism seemed like an ideal form of Christianity at that time in life because it provided a weekly scriptural "diet" of bible readings in easily digestible portions. And like rowing, it was beautifully choreographed. With the Book of Common Prayer, you could walk into Durham Cathedral, St. Chad's chapel, or any other church of its type the world over and sing the same hymns, hear the same epistles, and sit through the same sort of mercifully brief "homily" (short sermon). I always liked how these short sermons focused the hearer's attention on memorable take-away points.

If "High-Church" Anglicanism was one practice in England that differed from anything I experienced growing up, another were the weekly formal dinners in St. Chad's dining hall. The food was good, and the dress code was "smart" (as they called it): coat and tie for guys, and an equivalent for girls, with academic gowns for everyone, just like Harry Potter characters (the first movie of which happened to be filmed in Durham that very year). Each meal included a mild drinking ritual of sherry before dinner in the Senior Common Room, wine from the college cellar with dinner, port with dessert, and beer afterward in the college pub. This list makes the alcohol consumption seem heavy, which it certainly was, but at the time it didn't feel excessive because it was slowly paced.

Because very few Americans studied at Durham, I made good friends with two other Yanks: Mike at University College (nicknamed "Castle") and Ian at Hatfield. Of course, Mike and Ian would probably bridle at my calling them "Yanks" because they were both from Virginia. And both probably thought that being Virginian gave them a special understanding with the English that eluded northerners like me, which was may have been true. Since then, I've often observed that American southerners, with their cultural emphasis on politeness and indirect speech are much more "English" than mainstream Americans.

Each of our colleges had distinct reputations. Chad's was said to be quiet and studious; Castle was cultured and posh, and Hatfield was sporty and rowdy. Mike and Ian and I thought of Hatfield as Durham's Sparta, with the best-looking women and the most aggressive men. Alas, Hatfield women were certainly beautiful, but they always seemed unattainable, permanently ensconced in airtight cliques. When we invited each other to formal dinners at our respective colleges, they ran true to type. Chad's dinners were the most refined and culinary. Those at Castle the most archaic—with gothic-looking candles ablaze over a long oaken table on which they served messy dollops of potatoes, beef, and mystery veggies ground into a salty lumpy beige paste. It was the ugliest meal I ever had in England, which is saying something, but among the tastiest.

Hatfield formals were something altogether *different*. When Ian finally invited me to one, he told me to bring my own bottle of wine and to expect to finish it myself. This raised my antennae.

As we met outside Hatfield College that evening, I heard a distant thundering sound rumbling from the mess hall. When we got inside, a hundred students were dressed in academic gowns and banging their spoons on the tables in tribal cadence reminiscent of a Tarzan movie.

Before walking into the building, I had asked Ian why Hatfield students' academic gowns seemed to have food stains all over them, but now I understood as I saw dinner rolls flying from table to table, landing in soup bowls, hitting the floor, and knocking over glasses. Sure enough, everyone had a whole wine bottle to himself, and as people de-corked their bottles, they hurled the corks all around the dining hall—often at people's heads.

Then I noticed some people with carrots in their teeth who were passing the carrots off to their neighbors, mouth to mouth, until the same carrots passed all over the hall. Meanwhile, I stumbled upon one of their indigenous drinking games the hard way as someone leaned over and asked, "Do you know the rules of the game?" To which I (the victim) was prompted to reply, "It would be rude not to." Upon this answer, she dropped a coin into my wine, and I had to down the entire glass in one gulp. Before long, I could no longer feel my lips.

As everyone finished eating their meals, the "Senior Man" (the college version of a public-school prefect) leaped on a table, shouted some things that were unintelligible, and everyone cheered. As Ian recalls, "The senior man's comment would usually be an adolescent scatological joke, deliberately inappropriate for the setting." Then, instead of lingering at our seats over port, the way we would have done back at St. Chad's, everyone abruptly got up and made their way to the Hatfield College pub.

Here, the Senior Man grabbed a cane and started bashing it against a brass plate on the ceiling. Upon calling everyone to "order," everyone in the very crowded room started singing (shouting hoarsely at the tops of their lungs) the Beach Boys' song "Sloop John B" and variations rugby songs with accompanying pantomime motions known only to fully-fledged Hatfielders. After some of this, Ian clapped me on the back and said, "Come on, we're all going to Klute!"

Ah Klute, a Durham nightclub, much better experienced than described, housed in a ramshackle building under a bridge down by the river. If you looked at the ground outside for any length of time, you'd see rats scampering around boldly. There was a donner shop around the corner, nicknamed "the dirty shop," whose delicacies often wound up splattered on the pavement mixed with beery vomit.

The music at Klute was pure cheese, and it never changed. By that, I don't mean the *style* never changed, I mean the *exact songs* never changed, and they always seemed to be played in the exact same order. Now I think of it, the DJ may have simply had a fixed song list of sixties bubblegum pop, seventies glam rock, eighties power ballads, nineties gangster rap, and TV theme songs from *A-Team*; *Magnum, P.I.*; and *Knight Rider* that he played night after night without deviation. At the time, college tour guides comically described Klute as the "second-worst nightclub" in all of Europe. Apparently, since that time, Europe's "worst" nightclub (supposedly in Poland) is said to have burned down, leaving Klute the reigning champion.

I mention all this in such detail because there are many places like Klute. Dorrian's in New York, the 151 Club (a.k.a. "One-Dive-One") in London, and several equivalents in Hamburg immediately come to mind as examples. In every case, the uniting theme was simplicity and utter predictability. Ian and I summed all this all up as a thing called "civilized barbarity" – the chance to act wild within strict parameters. It's a tonic for counterbalancing the need to be disciplined, in control, and "on" so much of the time. Such pressure demands an equal chance to dance on tables, break glass, and sing at the top of your lungs to songs that came out when many people in the room were still in diapers.

The Preppy Virtues

Durham was a haven for all this. There were quite a few eccentrics running around who acted as if they were extras in *Brideshead Revisited*. Rumor had it that one guy in college called "Rob the Snob" provided his roommate free room and board the prior year in return for the roommate acting as his valet. Both were said to have enjoyed the arrangement.

Certainly, the vast majority of students at Durham were perfectly normal and utterly modern, but it's the eccentrics who stand out in memory. These aspects of life reminded me of what American Ivy league colleges must have been like before the 1950s—before SAT scoring switched educational emphasis from finishing school polishing to stricter scholastics (and "grade-grubbing").

66

Mike and Ian and I discussed this often. For example, at our Durham graduation, the guest speaker *deemphasized* scholarship as the main aim for graduate school. Instead he insisted that the main value of our university time didn't come from academic work with professors, but rather through casual friendships and extracurricular activities.

Today this reminds me of a 1979 *Atlantic Monthly* article in which Nelson Aldrich described a series of "preppy" virtues and charms which include:

> Deference
> Discretion
> Modesty
> Gratitude
> Grace

Let's consider each of these in turn, because they flesh out important aspects of the gentlemanly ideal.

Deference, "the ghost of chivalry," expresses a faith in "natural hierarchies of excellence" and sees goodness in yielding to authority.[27] It holds knowledge and seniority as worthy organizing principles for society. Crucially, deference emphasizes the *duties* we owe to others as opposed to insisting on the *rights* we demand from them. Instead of going around saying, "I know my rights," a deferential person asks, "What are my duties?" A

---

[27] "Nelson W. Aldrich on Preppies," Ivy Style, December 23, 2017, http://www.ivy-style.com/thirty-years-later-aldrich-on-preppies.html.

deferential person accepts that for every advantage you have over others, you also have equal responsibilities as well.[28]

Discretion is a form of theater, a social alertness "guided by gut instinct more than the intelligence or convention," in which you're ever alert for reverberations of your impact on others. It's a "sense of occasion," bordering on playacting, where you keep your eyes and ears tuned those around you. It allows you to trim your sails and move with tact.

Modesty is "the economy of egotism." Partly sincere and partly calculated to disarm envy, it honors others' claims to a share of the audience's time. "It's an awareness that, historically speaking, all feats are soon undone, surpassed, or shown to have had evil consequences." Modesty seeks to downplay *all* accomplishments—not just one's own. According to Nathaniel Burt, it "chastens the pride of those who are on the way up with the realization that others have been there before them."[29]

---

[28] Speaking chivalry, the following feudal terms are interesting to consider. The word *knight* is derived from *knecht*, a Germanic word for *servant*; the word *noble* describes someone of high social rank or high moral character; and *chivalry* is derived from the Norman word *chevalier*, which means *horseman*. String these together and you get a well-armed, well-heeled, well-bred horseman with good intentions who acts like servant.

[29] Nathaniel Burt, *The Perennial Philadelphians: The Anatomy of an American Aristocracy* (Boston: Little, Brown, 1963).

Gratitude expresses your dependence on others. It measures wealth *relationally* (who you know) as opposed to intellectually (what you know) or financially (what you have). Its currency is in "contacts, not in bank accounts." With gratitude In play, no one is ever allowed to think they've made it on their own: "While others might brag that they are self-made men, preppies [gentlemen] can only be grateful."

If you're grateful, it's easy to be *graceful*. Grace is the crowning trait of all the genteel charms, it's the tip of the pyramid. Grace accepts that we are all flawed, and that most people are doing the best they can with what they have. Grace forgives offenses and generously affords everyone with freedom to fail.

Grace is a matter of the heart, but there's also a bit of theatre to it. Aldrich defined this as "a languid, easy, uncalculating, nonchalant manner that embraces carelessness, negligence, indifference, and recklessness." Sometimes it takes effort to seem effortless. "Negligence requires attention, indifference requires concentration, simplicity and naturalness require affectation."

In other words, sometimes grace requires you to fake it till you make it, while letting others make their own mistakes along the way.

When you apply grace to competitive situations, you get *sportsmanship* which, as we saw earlier, holds that it's better to lose a game well than to win it badly. This naturally flows into the idea of *amateurism*, which holds that it's better to do things because you love them than to do them just for money. (Of course, it presupposes you have enough money to afford such a luxury.) Amateurism is what drove some of the American Founders to devote their lives and fortunes to forming a new government without accepting pay in return.

Dressing Like a Gentleman

The preppy virtues don't just relate to manners and behavior, but to grooming and personal appearance as well. Fearful of being too handsome, a gentleman needn't (shouldn't!) be perfect looking, but he should look have everything in working trim. He should seem like he has himself under control while having fun. Traditionally this implies a natural, clean-cut, soap-and-water aesthetic.

During my time in England, and later in Germany, clothing styles were fun to observe. In Europe people tended to dress much more formally than we often do in America, and I enjoyed that. Formality gave each day a better sense of occasion. It reminded me of basketball coach John Wooden's urge to "make each day your masterpiece."[30] It reminded me of what my grandfather once told me when I was a freshman in college, when he told me that students back in his day would always wear coat-and-tie to class. When I asked "Why?" he said "Respect!" "Respect for what?" I asked. "*Yourself*" he said.

In Durham, you'd often see people wearing sporty, classic things like rugby shirts, colorful school socks, and stuff from Ralph Lauren, Barbour, etc. in quite sloppy ways. For example, I recall one douchebag (I mean this as a term of endearment) who would wear untucked Thomas Pink dress shirts with unfastened French cuffs falling over his hands, collar popped

---

[30] https://www.thewoodeneffect.com/your-masterpiece/

(ironed into the UP position), with the front buttons undone to mid chest. granted, he was a special case, but there were quite a few similar examples. Of course, Durham had plenty of normally dressed students in the American sense who favored hoodies and sneakers, but in retrospect they are unmemorable.

In Heidelberg by contrast, students dressed much more carefully. One might even say "precisely." They were German after all, and Germans tend to be thorough ("grundlich"). Some guys and gals with preppy sensibilities went full bore on the "classic" look as they called it, wearing a timeless co-ed uniform of cashmere/ lambswool pullovers with dressy English shirts, his-and-her scarves, Barbour jackets, and smart shoes ranging in formality from moccasins to jodhpur boots and brogues. Ladies wore the same general rig with a feminine twist and jewelry, especially pearls. Some were amazingly fetching. For both sexes, sneakers were worn at the gym, not on Hauptsrasse.

Interestingly, in all the social environments I've encountered over the years (and there have been many), clothing tends to be *tribal* among guys. That is, regardless of nationality, age, or any other differentiator, guys may pretend to not care about clothes, but they all tended to dress exactly like their best friends.

How does all this apply to Americans dressing like gentlemen? Quite a bit. For over three hundred years, American gentlemen have worn "uniforms" based on London styles, which have remained amazingly unchanged over the years. By "unchanged" I don't mean that people still wear the stuff William Penn or John Winthrop wore in the 1600s; I mean that the *spirit* behind today's gentlemanly clothing is pretty much the same now as it was then.

According to Robert Claiborne, a buddy of mine who has been running high-end men's shops across the United States for decades,[31] there are gentlemen in every American region who favor (and even crave) proven, durable, and practical styles augmented with ample dashes of flair. The late President George H. W. Bush provides an example, with his thing for pairing somber J. Press sack suits and brightly colored socks.

Claiborne also noticed funny regional quirks nationwide. For example, he said that Philadelphia-area customers have a habit of buying more casual clothes for daily wear than guys would in cities like Boston or New York, but they favor much more formality for special occasions, which often include black and white tie. This is yet another playful balance between "plain" and "fancy."

Today, an American gentleman's "uniform" varies from region to region, but the general outfit includes things that have been in Brooks Brothers catalogues

---

[31] His shop is called *Claybourne's (The Gentleman's Clothier)*.

for generations: tailored suits of course, common-sense chinos and jeans, button-down shirts and polo shirts, blazers and sport coats, loafers and oxfords, dinner jackets (i.e. tuxedos), and a dozen other things available from shops like Brooks (the gold standard until Marks & Spencer nearly ruined them in the 1990s), J. Press (with styles reminiscent of early 1960s "ivy league" Pax Americana), the Andover Shop (fancy Bostonian), J.Crew (college boy), Ralph Lauren ("aspirational" fashion), Patagonia (outdoor smart aka "PataGucci"), L.L. Bean (cheap and good—a thrifty Philadelphia favorite), New & Lingwood (fancy-pants London), Ladage & Oelke (old-school Hamburg), Ben Silver (fancy Charleston) among many others. Almost anything featured in any book or article written about classical men's dress since the Kennedy administration is still up to date in some capacity. (Photos of JFK at home with his family demonstrate how timeless this aesthetic can be.) Old styles get constantly updated by wearing them with new twists and combinations.

Of course, none of this is carved in granite. An ever-evolving process occurs in the cannon as items which were once considered informal get slowly upgraded for more formal use. Gentleman's clothing is anchored in *history* but it's never stale. It celebrates an unbreakable connection with the past while remaining fresh and contemporary.

For example, tuxedo jackets which were once seen as a casual alternative to white-tie tailcoats are now among the most formal things you can wear, while today in New York City, guys are going to the office in welted work boots, narrow-loom blue jeans, and other things that counted as workwear for farm-hands in the 1930s. Meanwhile, business suits refuse to disappear as they get casually dressed down in new ways.

Military items have always been part of the mix. Like clockwork, they get added to the civilian cannon just as they fall out of tactical use on the battlefield. Similarly, athletic gear is gentlemanly in direct disproportion to its association with professional sports.

Crucially, gentlemen's dress obeys Kipling's insistence on "neither looking too good nor talking too wise." Even back in 1856 Emerson could say, "The Frenchman invented the ruffle, the Englishman added the shirt. The Englishman wears a sensible coat buttoned to the chin, of rough but solid and lasting texture. If he is a lord, he dresses a little worse than a commoner. They have diffused the taste for plain substantial hats, shoes, and coats through Europe. They think him the best dressed man, whose dress is so fit for his use that you cannot notice or remember to describe it."[32]

Along these lines, a 1938 *Life Magazine* article described how Princeton undergraduates set the tone for men's dress across the country: "The first

---

[32] Ralph Waldo Emerson, "English Traits: Ability."

thing a freshman learns is the importance of never looking 'dressed up' while always looking well-dressed." [33] The spirit behind this reminds me of a passage from the 1789 Episcopalian Book of Common Prayer, which said, "we [seek] to keep the happy mean between too much stiffness in refusing, and too much ease in admitting variations in things once advisedly established."[34] Today, whether a gentleman wears black-tie (tuxedo), coat and tie, or a fleece jacket and jeans, he still always strikes a line of being not too dressy while being well dressed.

To sum all this up (I could go on forever), a gentleman's *clothing* is just like his *manners*. It gives him dignity while making him comfortable—but not *too* comfortable, and it shows respect for himself and others. Poetically, we could say that classical men's clothing blends opposing complimentary couplets, such as:

- Beauty and Utility
- Town and Country
- Formality and Ease
- History and Modernity
- Thrift and Quality
- Snobbery and Equality
- Seriousness and Whimsy
- Comfort and Self-control

---

[33] Christian Chensvold, "The Rise and Fall of the Ivy League Look," http://www.ivy-style.com/the-rise-and-fall-of-the-ivy-league-look.html

[34] The Episcopal Church, *The Book of Common Prayer preface* (New York: Church Publishing Incorporated, 1979).

Finally, there's a tribal, familial aspect to all this that builds cohesion across the generations. The stability of gentlemanly dress creates a sense of belonging that's easy to cultivate for anyone who cares to do so. When a ten-year-old boy, forty-year-old dad, and seventy-year-old grandfather show up to an event wearing similar blazers, chinos, shirts, and shoes, it's a sartorial fountain of youth for the aging and an anchor for the young.

Etonians and *Wandervogel*

Midway through my year at Durham, my adviser asked what I would want to write about for my research dissertation. I said I might as well study how a single public school changed as a result of World War I. He liked the idea. At first, I wanted to focus on Harrow since Winston Churchill went there, but my adviser suggested Eton, and wrote a letter of introduction so I could search their archives.

The chance to visit Windsor (where Eton is) was a great opportunity for tourism. Upon hearing about my plans, people suddenly had all sorts of quips about the school. One guy called the *Eton College Chronicle* a "tabloid." Another joked, "If a lady requires a chair, an Etonian will *call for it*, a Wykehamist (Winchester guy) will *fetch it*, and a Harrovian will *sit in it* before she can."

The Eton archives were fascinating, run by a self-possessed woman called Penny whose quiet, firm demeanor was strangely electrifying. As she brought things out for me to read, she came alive and shared stories as I flipped through documents focusing on the World War I generation. These articles, many of which came from the *Eton College Chronicle*, helped me form a better image of Edwardian gentlemanliness. The main thing that jumped out was how militaristic Eton was. In that era just after the Boer War, it was fashionable for young men to serve in the army and navy.

Accordingly, there was a rich vein of sad material about talented young men who sacrificed their lives in various wars. After reading these stories, I started feeling guilty for not being in the military myself. Somewhat perversely, their hardships made me want to experience something similar myself, although preferably without getting killed.

At the very least, I suddenly wanted to go through basic training as a soldier, just as Plato described his young guardians doing in *The Republic*. For some reason, the thought learning how to use crew-served machine guns appealed to me greatly, along with marching and responding to commands. I've already mentioned all this in another book dedicated to that experience called *The Gentlemen of Gloucester*.

Back in Durham I had recently become friendly with an Etonian called Peter, who had just joined a cavalry unit in the British Army. He told me stories about life at Eton, about how remnants of the 19th century still remained in their brutal rugby games and how boys still needed to learn how to stand up to bullies. He also told me how, in his family the men always spent a few years in the army after college before going into the professions or banking.

It was interesting to see how Peter's views correlated with the guys I read about in the Eton archives. Seeing such a military tradition alive in Britain made me want to find my own version of it in America. It made me want to return home to join the US Marine Corps or something, perhaps as an intelligence officer.

But just as I started thinking about all this, a new person popped into my life who changed my trajectory completely. His name was Martin. He studied history at University College and came from Hamburg, the most Anglophile part of Germany. Like Gisela a few years earlier, Martin became another friend who greatly expanded my understanding of what it meant to be a gentleman.

As a Continental European, Martin prided himself on being a bit more "cultivated" than British students (who in turn seemed more cultivated than we Americans). He favored refinements and formalities that we might dismiss as affectations, but he counterbalanced these with a toughness he acquired through military experience in the German cavalry (armored reconnaissance). He spoke lavishly about his time in uniform, describing various life lessons acquired, which made me yearn to go home and join the military even more.

For example, he explained how the *Bundeswehr* (German army) taught him that big bureaucratic organizations are never monolithic. They may *seem* that way from a distance, but inside they're full of people with diverging interests and personalities. To navigate this sort of rabbit warren to get things done, he learned how to grease the wheels by giving people gifts, and he learned to play people with strong personalities against each other when they made trouble. He insisted that *bureaucratic skills* were essential for any gentleman because gentlemen must be able to operate equally well in vast organizations, just as they need to be team players in small groups. He said there's an art to both.

In a way, Martin's version of gentility reminded me of things described in *The Book of the Courtier*, a "courtesy book" written in 1528 by Baldassare Castiglione that dealt with etiquette, behavior, and morals for people in princely and royal courts.

The book was famous in Elizabethan times when the Italians represented all things subtle, polished, and artistic to the English (just as the Greeks had once done for the Romans, and as the English would later do for Americans). Castiglione wrote about manners, cultivation, and virtue at the same time Niccolò Machiavelli wrote about power manipulation in his more famous work *The Prince*. To emphasize the gentlemanly perspective, we'll cast Machiavelli aside in favor of Castiglione.

Castiglione described the ideal courtier as a nobleman with a cool mind and well-trained body who would dress well and speak in a smooth voice neither too effeminate nor too rough. He would try to perform difficult tasks as if they were easily done. He would be an excellent soldier, avid sportsman, and accomplished artist, and yet also be funny, modest, and kind. In short, Castiglione insisted that a courtier should be an "all-rounder."

His insistence on versatility over specialization put a stamp on the gentlemanly idea that remains in force today, and which Martin certainly cultivated. It's the root of such sayings as "A gentleman should know something about *everything* and everything about *something*" or "The world is run by C+ students" or "Straight A students work for C+ students," the idea being that people who get straight A's in school tend to do well in controlled, predictable environments but they can't adapt to environments where external forces bring "creative destruction."

The Wandervogel

Martin's military stories fascinated me, but he also had another set of experiences that caught my attention as well. As a kid he had been a member of the *Wandervogel* (which in German means "wandering bird"), a youth organization somewhat like the Boy Scouts but *much* more bohemian. In the German Romantic tradition, the Wandervogel hitchhiked all over Europe, ranging far and wide, carrying guitars on their shoulders to sing for food, sleeping in farmers' haylofts and open fields, and fording streams with rucksacks stripped down to their boxer shorts.

At first, I didn't believe Martin's claims about having hitchhiked as a kid in Germany. To my American mindset the idea was absurd. But he soon proved his salt by strong-arming me into hitchhiking with him from Durham to London to visit a friend. He dragged me to a gas station outside town. After waiting a while, a van full of hippies pulled up. He approached them winsomely and asked if we might join them wherever they were going (which happened to be London). We hopped in, did our best to make small talk, and reached Martin's friend's house in London by nightfall.

The friend was a professor at University College London. He seemed "old" at the time (middle 30s!) and looked like a blonde version of Hugh Grant and may well have been a devil with the ladies. That night, I told him and Martin about my plan to join the marines, but they strongly advised against it. Martin convinced me to postpone the marines for a visit to Heidelberg, where he had once studied. Again, I've already described how this transpired (sleeping under a bridge my first night in Germany) in *The Gentlemen of Gloucester*, but there's much more to the story than I mentioned in that book.

By interrupting my military plans, Martin delayed one aspect of my gentlemanly education by supplementing another: foreign language through *immersion*.

Moving to a country where they don't speak your language messes with your brain and makes the easiest normal tasks feel *impossible*. You lose all sense of control. In my case, simple things like opening door locks, figuring out how European shower fixtures worked, and ordering food at restaurants baffled me. Worn out from thinking in odd new patterns, I'd often sit on park benches in a daze.

Through amazing good fortune however, I randomly met an American living in Heidelberg who arranged for me to sleep on a mattress in the hallway of his student apartment for the following month. By living with a group of students, I got the chance to experience daily life with people who spoke a foreign language. It was all very exciting.

While I was navigating life with these new German acquaintances, Martin called out of the blue from England to put me in touch with his own circle of friends, which suddenly gave me access to several cliques at once. Some of these people were outdoorsy types from the Wandervogel. Others were fraternity guys who belonged to an old student corps similar to Yale's Skull and Bones or Princeton's Ivy Club. Others were pot-heads my American buddy knew. (These varied groups expanded my *social range* quite drastically. If grace is one of the keystones of gentility, social range ranks equally important. Neither of these traits come easily. They can only be cultivated with practice.)

One day, Martin's brother invited me to join his Wandervogel friends on a weekend "tramping" (hitchhiking) trip. But this wasn't just any old hitchhiking trip. This outing they had strict rules, making it something of a game. According to the rules, each guy had to hitchhike from wherever he lived in Germany to an agreed-upon rally point in some village whose name I now forget.

As "tramps," we couldn't bring any camping equipment: no rucksack, no sleeping bag, no tent—not a single luxury. "But what if it rains?" I asked. "We get wet," he deadpanned like an Apache chief. We could carry whatever we could stuff into our pockets—but nothing more. The outing would last from Friday night through Sunday.

Thrilled with this bizarre challenge, I threw myself into the wind with minimal preparation. I dressed in several layers (not nearly enough, as it turned out) and crammed as much food as I could into the pockets of my Filson tin-cloth jacket.

Martin's brother Micha and his buddy York agreed to babysit me. They took me to the rally point near whatever village it was. As we arrived, other Wandervogel old-boys were already there—Martin's original gang from the 1990s who were now in their late twenties and early thirties. They all seemed "old" to me at the time and were obviously very good friends.

As the evening sunlight faded, more of them arrived, dropped off by passing cars in the gathering dusk. They shook hands and caught up on friendly gossip, and sat down in the chilly October night, pulling things from their pockets to eat. This began one of the quickest and most memorable lessons in gentlemanliness I've ever experienced.

The lesson? Sharing your food. As I pulled sausage and cheese from my pockets, intending to gobble them up myself (in the American spirit of rugged individualism), I noticed that none of the others took a scrap from his own pocket without first offering it to everyone else. That is, no one took a single bite of his own food. Each offered it to the others, expecting the others to share theirs in turn. And when the others ate, they didn't just take polite little bites as a gesture—they took *real* bites, gobbling it all down.

Anyone who shared his food with the rest of the group could be sure there wouldn't be any left for himself. But since everyone brought equal amounts of food and shared it with everyone else equally liberally, the system miraculously worked. It tapped into a tradition of German "communalism" alien to Anglo-Saxon thought. (I use the term "Anglo-Saxon" here as the French use it, to describe all people on earth for whom English is their native tongue.)

Thus trapped, I reluctantly pulled a sumptuous sausage from my pocket I'd been looking forward to eating, gave it to the guy on my right, and kissed it goodbye.

The next two days passed in a blur, at times miserable and at times euphoric. We hiked through country roads soaking in the sun by day, wandering from village to village, singing old Wandervogel songs in the streets at night to beg for food. At one point someone gave us money for beer, and we each got a few cans.

With nowhere better to go, we slept in a market square that first night. And it was very cold. I "inhaled" my two cans of beer, hoping to ward off the chill, but woke up shivering within half an hour, cowed in a shallow doorway trying to cover up with stray pieces of cardboard. As Fitzroy McClean said while describing a much more painful episode in the North African desert, "Time passed slowly." I returned to Heidelberg feeling like a much wiser man, but when I tried to describe the tramping trip to friends in the student apartment, words failed me.

Two Finishing Schools

After my first month in Heidelberg, Martin introduced me to Yvonne (not her real name), a German student who studied French and English. He thought we might be good study partners to improve our English and German respectively, and he was right. She soon became my girlfriend. Within weeks of meeting her, life accelerated. I found a job locally, which allowed me to stay in Heidelberg for the next two years, and Yvonne helped me find an apartment.

Yvonne was a magnificent woman by any stretch. She was exactly age (twenty-five at the time), exactly height (just under 5'10"), and roughly my weight, but much better educated, much better bred, and much more intelligent than I. In short, she was just the sort of challenging person from whom I could learn a lot. In a much stronger (Teutonic) way than Gisela, Yvonne became a one-woman "finishing school" for addressing my rough edges.

Being German, her rules for behavior were much stricter than Gisela's Dutch customs. (To give an idea of the difference, Yvonne preferred notebooks with vertical *and* horizontal lines, because mere horizontal lines failed to provide enough "order"). Over the course of our time together, Yvonne pointed out countless flaws in my manners that my parents and grandparents had never been able to change in me.

Daily life as a couple was challenging, and whenever I was at her place, I didn't handle domesticity well. We spent most evenings together doing normal things couples do, like eating dinner, watching TV, or going shopping. Time and again, she had to remind me not to leave dishes in the sink without washing them, not to drip wine on the tablecloth whenever I poured a glass (her poor yellow table cloth looked like a kid with the measles thanks to all the wine drops I spilled), not to leave kitchen cabinets open after using them, not to make sandwiches on the countertop without using a plate, not to leave the toilet seat up, and so on.

Obviously, my mom harped on all things when I was a kid, but I rebelled against them and intentionally *unlearned* them as a college freshman when life suddenly became free. But Yvonne's bootcamp was valuable. Her best advice was the following phrase, which she often repeated: *Don't make work for other people.*

Once, when I complained that she treated me like a child, she said, "I'll treat you like an adult whenever you start acting like one." Ultimately of course, this all worked for my good: "As iron sharpens iron, one person sharpens another."

Classical good manners tied into what Yvonne was getting at. Some of these timeless "dos and don'ts" for gentlemen are worth reiterating for younger generations, because society often conspires to erode them. The basics include:

- Make eye contact when greeting people.
- Remove your hat indoors.
- Always remove your glove before shaking someone's hand (people who know this rule seem to really appreciate when others know it).
- If you're seated, hop to your feet when a lady or senior person approaches you.
- Eat elegantly with knife and fork.
- Send hand-written thank-you notes whenever someone treats you to something nice.
- If you drink socially, don't get drunk.
- Don't make romantic overtures from which the other person can't retreat with dignity.[35]

As Yvonne got me thinking about traditional manners in new ways, I realized they are both *practical* and *beautiful*. And they're especially helpful for dealing with people in *groups*. In group situations, formal manners allow people to be nice and warm to each other while also keeping cool. They restrain spontaneous demonstrations of feeling by giving them customary channels of expression.[36] They provide a "playbook" for subordinating your selfish impulses for the good of the group.

---

[35] There's a great little book about this called *To Manner Born, To Manners Bred*, a hip-pocket manual for undergraduates at Hampden-Sydney College in Virginia. Another one is George Washington's *Rules of Civility and Decent Behaviour in Company and Conversation*, available at museum gift shops.

[36] Rupert Wilkinson, *Gentlemanly Power: British Leadership and the Public School Tradition* (London: Oxford University Press, 1964).

Love Your Neighbor As Yourself

Of course, good traditional manners are rooted in something that was quickly summed up in the second half of Jesus' main law for his disciples: "Love your neighbor as yourself."

Love is a bold word to throw around, so what did Jesus mean by this precisely? The apostle Paul elaborated with this description: "Love is patient, love is kind. It does not envy, it does not boast, it is not proud. It does not dishonor others, it is not self-seeking, it is not easily angered, it keeps no record of wrongs. Love does not delight in evil but rejoices with the truth. It always protects, always trusts, always hopes, always perseveres" (1 Cor. 13:4–7 NIV). If we tease this into a list, we get an operating system for manners, which trumps anything ever written by Emily Post:

> Be patient
> Be kind
> Don't envy others
> Don't boast
> Don't be proud
> Don't dishonor others
> Seek other's welfare, not just your own
> Avoid getting angry
> Don't keep track of wrongs
> Don't delight in evil
> Seek the truth and speak the truth
> Seek to protect others (and yourself)
> Dare to hope, and strive to persevere

Learning German — and Empathy

It was hard to have a social life in Germany that first year when my language skills weren't very good. Yvonne would take me out with her friends to all sorts of events, and at dinner parties, morning brunches, and fraternity all-nighters, I spent hours and hours surrounded by chattering, laughing, bantering people speaking German when I couldn't string a single sentence together.

Trying to keep up, I laughed when others laughed, and tried not to look bored when I spent hours not understanding what anyone was saying. Sometimes it was so frustrating I literally felt like crying. It took me a long time to break the language barrier.

But this was also a good lesson for gentlemanliness. It taught me about the need of empathy for foreigners, best summed up by this verse in Deuteronomy: "And you are to love those who are foreigners, for you yourselves were foreigners in Egypt" (10:19 NIV). Such empathy is especially crucial for American gentlemen because we are a nation of immigrants.

Money

At this point it's worth breaking some personal mores to mention something I was brought up not to talk about publicly: *money*. During most of my time in England and Germany I was strapped for cash. In other words, I don't want to give the impression that I was dancing through Europe on a trust fund. Far from it.

Durham ate into much of my savings and Heidelberg, though I often had a job, was fiscally catastrophic. The company I worked for, which ran computer training courses for US government personnel in Europe, hit the skids during 2001–2003 (my years in Germany) because of the war in Iraq. Eventually I quit that job and found roadie work on a staging crew setting up product displays for the Swiss automation company ABB at business conventions around Germany. This helped keep the wolf from the door — somewhat.

Yvonne helped tremendously. She chipped in by finding me an extremely cheap apartment in an attic at an old house where I shared a bathroom with another tenant who was just a step off the street himself. His room emitted noxious fumes of infrequent laundering and stale cigarette smoke, and he coughed so violently at night that I often expected any one of those racking fits to be his last. But as I said, the place was mercifully cheap.

Yvonne's dad owned a factory or something that was presumably well-sorted, but he seemed to keep her on a tight leash financially. So, we both found ourselves strapped for cash and occasionally singing the blues. One day when I was really down, she said, "Let's take the money we would normally use to eat for two days and splurge instead on a massive brunch at Weisser Bock (a great restaurant in Heidelberg)." And splurge we did. A magnificent brunch. Nearly twenty years on, I can still remember that brunch when I've forgotten its cost long ago.

Hard financial straits forced me to consider Jesus' parable about God and mammon, in which he described how each person has choice to either master money or let it master you.

He said, "No one can serve two masters. Either you will hate the one and love the other, or you will be devoted to the one and despise the other. You cannot serve both God and money" (Matt. 6:24 NIV). In Germany I was forced to develop a form of "financial courage" to thriftily skate by, hoping that what I was learning in life was more valuable than what I might otherwise be earning on a more conventional path back home. In the end, it was a matter of prioritizing *experiences* over *possessions*.

Fraternity

While Yvonne was chipping away at my "delinquent male" flaws on a steady basis from her female perspective, in Heidelberg I also had exposure to a male "finishing school" as well. I befriended some guys in a student corps that was similar to the Dutch fraternity Gisela had once told me about. The German version's founding members originally came from Saxony and Prussia in the east.

Their families had once been knights in the Middle Ages and they held vast tracts of land up until the 1940s. They abandoned these properties as the Soviets advanced at the end of World War Two, escaping to the west as "fluechtlinge" (refugees). Forced to start over from scratch, they were salted with a mix of residual pride and deep humility. In certain ways the younger generations carried strains of their ancient cultural inheritance into modern life.

Without realizing it, they demonstrated how families can transfer their culture over the generations while resisting influences of general society around them. They taught me various tiny little things about European nobility which Alexis de Tocqueville described in *Democracy in America*. Much of this is difficult to describe in words today, but it was palpable for me in person back then.

Medieval knighthood, like the American Cowboy myth, provides a foundation for the gentlemanly ideal rooted more in romance than fact. Both knightly and cowboy images involve tough guys on horseback with honor codes backed by raw killing power. Both involve chivalry with strict rules for how to treat adversaries, comrades, and women. Although both images are somewhat fantastical, they are rooted enough in fact to provide compelling standards for manhood in real life. Like Yvonne, these fraternity guys had certain rules of behavior that seemed like a modern sort of chivalry to me.

For example, when sitting with women at dinner, you had to constantly watch their wineglasses and water glasses to make sure they were filled. You had to be vigilant in case they wanted anything. Ever ready to jump up from your seat if one them rose to leave, or if a new person arrived. At the dinner table, a lady's every wish was your command.

If she pulled out a cigarette, you'd better have a lighter in your pocket at the ready. The moment she pulled out a smoke, you'd have to snap a flame and hold it *above* her eye level, so as she leaned up to light her cigarette, her hair would fall back away from her face and away from the flame.

Sometimes when meeting older ladies, you'd have to click your heels and bow your torso slightly for a quick hand kiss. At formal events you had to know ballroom dancing as well as a German version of 1950s rock-and-roll dancing called Knottentanz (literally "knot-dancing") which seemed like something from the movie *Grease*. (I've since learned that Americans down South have something similar called "swag.") Yvonne brought me up to speed with lots of these things and the Saxon-Prussians reinforced them.

It eventually dawned on me that many of the manners that felt so formal in Germany 2003 were not that different from what my grandparents' generation practiced in America before World War II—back before the 1960s "countercultural revolution" tried to sweep them away. From that perspective, it didn't seem like the Germans were so strict, but that we Americans had fallen so far.

On the Road Again

Although I liked Heidelberg very much, I knew I couldn't stay there forever. I had my own roots near Philadelphia, and though Pennsylvania seemed like the most boring place on earth when I was growing up, I slowly came to realize how much it really had to offer. Also, I still felt a compelling need to join the military...

Before wrapping things up to head home, I decided to do an extended trip through Germany to visit some of the friends I'd accumulated over the prior two years. With eight weeks to burn before Christmas, I knew enough people to sofa surf for a while.

Because hitchhiking was much more accepted in Germany than it was in the United States, I met plenty of people who encouraged me in this plan and offered advice. One guy said, "You should never carry a tent while wandering, because [not having one] forces you to be creative in finding places to sleep. When you have a tent, you pitch your tent night after night—where's the fun in that? But when you bivouac [sleeping in the open], you're forced to improvise."

Eager to break from Heidelberg's gravitational pull, I spent my last few nights in town camping on a wooded hillside opposite the city on the Neckar River, where Martin had once told me it was safe to drink from streams. It made me smile to think that I was now leaving Heidelberg just as I had arrived: sleeping under a bridge. Having vacated my apartment I slept under an overpass that last night and awoke the next morning to a pile of dog shit near my head, while birds chirped, and river barges passed majestically by. I stowed my things, and then spent hours mindlessly circling around town on my bicycle, feeling like a goldfish in a bowl. It was time to leave.

On this final trip, I would sometimes take trains and sometimes hitchhike. After hitchhiking with others so often, it felt amazing to do it on my own without supervision. On one occasion, one of Martin's Wandervogel friends dropped me off at an autobahn gas station, and I quickly got a ride with a Danish truck driver. The Wandervogel had taught me that trucks were a "compromise" choice for hitchhiking because they were slower than cars but offered grander views: "To sit high up in the passenger seat, seeing the world through the flat-fronted bay window of an LKV [tractor trailer], all of Europe is open to you."

Although it's easy to associate hitchhiking with vagabonds and serial killers, it's also one of the most gentlemanly experiences imaginable — in the British schoolboy adventurous sense. It forces you to stay in the moment while also planning ahead. You constantly map out your route, figuring how to get from A to B to C while considering alternate routes in case the driver should take an unexpected turn.

While keeping your eye on the route so the driver can let you off at the right gas station, you also have to make conversation with him, calculating why he picked you up in the first place. Did he want someone for conversation to keep him entertained? Does he want you to just sit there and shut up? Is he an ax murderer? Is she a lonely woman looking for love? A gentleman all-rounder must be ready for anything. *Be Prepared,* as Lord Baden-Powell taught the Boy Scouts.

If hitchhiking had its highs, it also had tremendous lows. When you go for even a short stretch of time without getting a ride or meeting nice people to talk with, the whole world can seem like it's arrayed against you. Life seems like a photo negative in which all the darks and lights are reversed. One moment you feel like a hero, and the next you feel like a bum—because in many ways, you *are* a bum.

But it's amazing how wandering around like a vagabond, ostensibly free of routines, creates its own routines. You start noticing recurring periods while underway: exploring new places, talking at length with strangers, making do when you're alone, finding places to bivouac at night. Whenever I reached a new town, I'd often pick an agreeable looking bar or café and sit there for a few hours, making myself at home, chiming in on random conversations within earshot and reading things in German to improve my vocabulary.

It was amazing how much more quickly my language skills improved on the road than they did in Heidelberg. Back in Heidelberg, the people who knew me would always correct my German whenever I made mistakes. Although they did this trying to be helpful, by only focusing on my mistakes, they eroded my confidence to take risks. By contrast, when I was on the road, strangers were so impressed that I knew any German at all that they showered me with compliments for the negligible language skills I did have, which boosted my confidence and allowed me to blossom.

This taught me a crucial gentlemanly/ educational principle that I'm still honing today: Praise people for what they *can* do. Don't nitpick what they can't. And be just as generous with yourself. When excellence is the goal, perfectionism is the enemy.

Thar She Blows

Around that time, a "ghost" started haunting me from the past—the ghost of dear old Gisela, the Dutch exchange student who captured my heart back in college. Her impact on me never quite went away. And now three years on, it was odd to be in Europe knowing she was breathing air on the same continent. Ever since meeting her, learning from her, loving her, and getting emotionally cauterized in the bargain, she set a high-jumping bar that no other woman could clear.

Back in Heidelberg, I once made the mistake of mentioning her to Yvonne in passing, and Yvonne reacted violently: "You're obviously still in love with that Dutch girl!" she said. "I've never seen you look at *anyone* the way you just smiled when you mentioned her name." She continued, now in a sisterly way, "Listen, if you care about this chick as much as you obviously seem to, you need to find her in Holland to see if anything's there. Maybe her feelings for you have changed since you were in college."

I recoiled at this suggestion, because the scars still ran deep—I felt like one of those manatees you see in National Geographic whose back has been gouged by a boat propeller. But I knew Yvonne was right. And I knew that Gisela was finishing medical school in Rotterdam just then. Visiting her would take courage. But why not? It was worth a shot.

In a way, Gisela had long ago ceased to be an actual "person" in my memory. She'd become more of a symbol. A symbol of *defeat*, like Waterloo or Custer's Last Stand. In fact, she became for me what the great white whale was for Captain Ahab in *Moby Dick*. Poor old Ahab, the great white whale bit off his leg, and for the rest of his life he could never rest knowing the whale was still "out there," *somewhere*, in some dark distant ocean waiting to be harpooned.

Of course, Gisela hadn't eaten my leg. But she shared some traits with Moby Dick, as far as I was concerned. She was certainly pale, and large (tall at least), and "out there," somewhere... Who knew? Maybe she was swimming around in Rotterdam waiting for me to strike with Cupid's harpoon.

So (according to my journal) on Friday, 21 November 2003, I hitchhiked from Frankfurt to Bergen op Zoom, some town in Holland. A woman driver took me a few gas stations beyond that place, and then a guy from Italy picked me up and dropped me off near Aachen, and then a Czech couple took me to Rotterdam, where I tucked into a café bar, to record some things in my journal while nursing a beer.

That night I bivouacked outside in the rain, wrapped in a tarp with multiple clothing layers on to attempted warmth. Let me tell you, there was *nothing* romantic about tramping *that* night. That night I felt like an *actual* vagabond—unbathed, unwanted, and seedy. This feeling fed on itself as I imagined Gisela somewhere that very night at some cozy Dutch pub, bantering away with impossibly attractive friends like the ones I'd seen years before on that Ralph Lauren–ad hunting day.

Were there any gentlemanly lessons to draw that miserable night? Just that verse from Deuteronomy: "And you are to love those who are foreigners, for you yourselves were foreigners in Egypt."

I forget precisely how I made it to Amsterdam the next day, but when I got there Gisela called my cell phone inviting me to a bar where she and her family were celebrating her brother's birthday. When I found the bar, I stared at the door for a while screwing up my courage like a man waiting for the whistle to go over the top at Gallipoli. In I walked, and at once they were all in view—her whole charming family—along with a gaggle of other people who instantly blurred away from my vision. The scene was, as the Dutch say, *gezellig* (cozy).

The instant Gisela saw me, she dropped what she was doing and came running over, flailing her arms to balance on stiletto heels that transformed her from six feet tall to six three. Gushing and babbling, she said, "Oh, *Drew*! So good to finally *see* you! I can't *believe* it! You look *exactly* the same as before!" (That comment annoyed me: Hadn't I just spent three years transforming from a caterpillar into a butterfly?) She interrupted herself, "Oh, *gee*! So *stupid* of me. I *never* wear high heels! Only tonight for the birthday... So stupid of me since *you* were coming," she said, looking down at me beaming with her hands planted on her hips like Wonder Woman.

All day I had been promising myself that Gisela would be a faded version of the gorgeous exchange student I knew at Millersville University. But here she was, much better than before. A bit harder looking perhaps, a bit gaunter. Less naivete certainly. No trace of the farmer's daughter anymore. But without a doubt the prettiest woman I'd ever seen—on or off the screen.

When we sat down, she lifted a drink from the bar and absentmindedly jammed herself in the eye with the straw. "Me again!" she laughed. She had always been prone to such gaffes, just like Inspector Clouseau in *Pink Panther*.

Although I didn't expect us to have much to say, we blabbed away effortlessly just like that first bike ride to Lancaster. The butterflies disappeared from my stomach, my fear evaporated, and I thought, "This is what true love must really feel like." It seemed obvious—yet again—that we were made for each other.

She invited me to visit her in Rotterdam, and we met a few days later for dinner. This time however, things were different. As I looked across the table, she seemed tired and worn from having just completed a hospital shift. She wore frumpy scrubs and coke-bottle glasses instead of contact lenses (she had eyes like a bat). Compared to her beauty-queen appearance in Amsterdam days earlier, she now seemed drab. But this homelier appearance made me love her all the more—it reminded me that I liked her not just for how she looked on the *outside* but for who she was *inside*.

At first that evening went swimmingly. We clicked into gear, talking about anything and everything. As often before, our thoughts matched pace and we finished each other's sentences before the words came out. At one point she called me her "alter ego" because we had so much in common.

But then the figurative phonograph needle screeched. She asked if I were dating anyone and I said NO thinking, "Dear thing, she's checking my availability to make sure I'm single!" Telepathically sensing the tone of my answer, she quickly corrected any misunderstanding I might have about her intentions by launching into an enthusiastic description of her love life that semester, which involved multiple guys and ample amour.

At first, I couldn't believe what I was hearing. Then as it registered, my stomach turned. My blood ran cold (I could feel it draining from my face), and I nearly wanted to vomit.

She noticed my reaction and instantly understood how her words had affected me. But instead of pulling back, she roundhouse kicked me in the chest by explaining that although she loved me as a "friend" (vile word), she could never love me romantically—in case that was still on my mind.

As this soaked in, it occurred to me that in *Moby Dick* the great whale ultimately *killed* Captain Ahab. My enthusiasm for spending another moment with Gisela leaked through the floor.

But there was more to come.

As I mentioned earlier, Dutch people love bicycles and they generally look dashing while riding them. They use bikes for pleasure and basic transportation like the Maoist Chinese. So, after dinner, we walked outside, and Gisela unlocked her bike. Gesturing to it, she said, "We'll have to share my bike to ride home. I'll go sidesaddle on the rear rack because I'm the girl, and you can pedal up front because you're the man." (She'd always been a staunch anti-feminist when it came to gender roles.)

Given this fleeting chance to salvage my pride, I straddled the bike and tried to steady it as she hopped on the back. But I was in poor physical shape that year and (more importantly) had never ridden a bike with a person on the back before. Let me tell you, trying to balance a Dutch roadster with the saddle too high while a six-foot woman throws her weight on the back feels like trying to right a capsizing Harley. After a few times of trying and failing, Gisela shook her head at me and said, "It's no use. Let's switch." And I had no choice but to comply.

She straddled the bike and stabilized it with practiced ease as I pitifully wedged myself on the rear rack. She told me to hold her waist and then pushed off, standing up on the peddles to pump the bike up to speed. As we glided back to her apartment in silence through traffic on the rain-wet Rotterdam streets, my humiliation was complete.

Did that night teach me anything about being a better gentleman? Yes. (I guess.) It reminded me of that line from Kipling:

> *If you can meet with Triumph and Disaster*
> *and treat those two impostors just the same.*

That night taught me something else about gentlemanliness in the macho Victorian sense that I had too long overlooked: the need for raw physical strength. Many of my role models—the ancient Israelites (King David and his "mighty men of valor"), the ancient Greeks, the medieval knights, the early American pioneers, and the farm boys and steel workers who manned the infantry in World War II—they all faced a need for general endurance and occasional brute force.

After all, if a gentleman must first be a man before he can be gentle, and he might as well to be *strong*. Intellectually, emotionally, and spiritually of course, but also physically. Not Arnold Schwarzenegger strong, but soldier strong, construction-worker strong, carry-a-wounded-comrade strong, make-someone-sorry-they-picked-on-you strong.

Although swimming and rowing made me aerobically fit, that night in Rotterdam showed me some new areas for improvement. As Carl von Clausewitz wrote in his masterpiece *On War*, the most basic of all strategies is to be as strong as possible—first in general and then at the decisive point.[37] This would become a major life priority that I continue to work on today.

[37] Carl von Clausewitz, *On War* (Princeton University Press: 1989).

First Troop Philadelphia City Cavalry

After finishing my trip through Germany, I returned to Pennsylvania for Christmas in 2003, aiming to join the military. The US had just invaded Iraq. Although I was generally apolitical back then, I *did not* agree with the war. The idea of invading a sovereign country with "preemptive war" seemed appalling. It reminded me of when ancient Rome drifted from being a republic to becoming an empire. Not only did the Iraq invasion seem like our version of crossing the Rubicon, it bothered me that our country, founded on the idea of citizen-soldier militia, was now hiring mercenaries to fight. And it especially vexed me to imagine politicians and policy planners in Washington voting for a war in which other people's children would die when they themselves had avoided serving in the 1960s.

Therefore, enlisting in the army became not just a romantic urge to develop personal character of the type I read about in the Eton archives, it became a way for me feel like an American citizen worthy of the Founding Fathers.

I should back up by mentioning that when I was still living in Heidelberg, I discovered a Pennsylvania Army National Guard unit called the First Troop Philadelphia City Cavalry (hereafter referred to as the *Troop*), an idiosyncratic organization founded in 1774 that still operates as a dual-purpose combat unit and ceremonial outfit.

To paraphrase what I've already written about the Troop in *The Gentlemen of Gloucester*, its original organizers were members of the Gloucester Fox Hunting Club (America's first subscription hunt, founded in 1766). As entrepreneurs and financiers, they pledged to serve Congress without pay as mounted reconnaissance soldiers and dispatch riders, serving as General Washington's personal bodyguard at the battles of Trenton, Princeton, and Germantown. Decades after the revolution, the Troop became a foundational building block for the Pennsylvania National Guard, as well as a social organization connected with the city's oldest clubs. Today, the Troop still serves its original intended purpose, operating out of an armory building in the Rittenhouse section of Philadelphia.

Because it predates the US Army, the Troop has "ancient rights and privileges" under the Constitution, allowing it to elect its own officers and wear its own ceremonial uniform (designed by the Marquis de Lafayette in 1824).

When I discovered the Troop in 2003, it had some remarkable customs. One of these was "rank flip-flopping," in which members would willingly take reductions in rank to serve in the unit. For example, Robert Wharton famously did this in the eighteenth century when he joined the Troop as a private, rose to the rank of captain, advanced to brigadier general in the Pennsylvania militia, and then became mayor of Philadelphia. When the War of 1812 broke out, Wharton reenlisted back into the unit as a *private*.

111

Although Wharton's story was an extreme case, the tradition remained in the twenty-first century.

By 2003, the organization seemed exclusive at first glance, but in reality (like most old-school organizations) they were eagerly looking for new members. Their recruiting woes came from simple math: few officer-quality college students wanted to enlist in the army as privates, and few normal army privates wanted to adopt "stuffy" Old Philadelphian customs, donate their drill pay, and wear tight pants riding horseback down Chestnut Street. This equation made the unit quite accessible to anyone who wanted to play the game.

The guys who gravitated to the Troop tended to be somewhat romantic (you think?) and not easily pigeonholed. Each walked to his own beat. Many were educated at good colleges and prep schools, but quite a few weren't. Some were lawyers or bankers who wanted to some adventure to their lives; others were tradesmen and Philly cops.

Politically speaking, they ranged from very conservative to very liberal. Differing opinions were absolutely encouraged, and people could remain friends while violently disagreeing on any range of issues. These days the American media divides the US into two camps—red states and blue states. But Troopers were a mix of both. They were *purple*.

The Troop's governance was especially interesting from the standpoint of gentlemanly education, because it was *both* a top-down military hierarchy and a bottom-up representative democracy with monthly meetings run according to Robert's Rules of Order. This provided members with a chance to hone their experience in rhetoric—one of the skills Plato recommended for his "guardians". As one man described this mix of hierarchy and equality, "When we're in uniform, we're army. The commander becomes the commander. But when we're at the Armory in civilian clothes, we're a democracy, and the commander gets called by his first name."

This odd dynamic made the Troop a de facto leadership training school. Not in a directive way, but in a persuasive way. Everyone occasionally wanted to be the boss, and no could ever really dominate anyone else. Getting people to act in concert was like herding cats. But isn't that how Americans are generally?

According to one older Trooper, "If you get too assertive in this organization, others will resist you, because no one wants anyone else to get too big for his britches. So, if you want to take initiative, you must choose your battles *very* carefully. Never take on too much. You've got to plan things out well in advance, and then act as *quickly* and *quietly* as possible. If it works out, no one will ever thank you for it. And if you screw up, they'll *hang* you." Such rules probably apply to any volunteer fire company, condo association, or any other small organization in which, as they say, "The politics are so high because the stakes are so low."

All these factors (and many more) made the Troop an ideal place to continue developing as an American gentleman of the Philadelphia variety. Europe may have refined me a bit, but now I had to relax back into being a regular Pennsylvanian. In a sense, the Troop was yet another "finishing school," just as Durham and Heidelberg were. Only this time around, the emphasis was on *toughening up*.

I enlisted in the National Guard as a cavalry scout, and it seemed like quite a job. In the US Army, "cav scouts" are trained to operate beyond the front lines without being detected, and to communicate enemy movements back to higher command. In *Boots on the Ground*, a book about the 2003 Iraq invasion, Karl Zinsmeister said, "For cavalry troopers, it's almost impossible to re-create within a training exercise the free-floating, slash-and-burn buccaneering that combat brings."[38]

---

[38] Karl Zinsmeister, *Boots on the Ground* (New York: Truman Talley Books, 2003).

Basic Training

My next step was to attend basic training at Fort Knox, Kentucky. This was daunting, but exciting, because I saw it as a chance to undergo the sort of crucible experience that fascinated me so much about the Victorian public schools.

At basic training, the army washes you of your past and gives you a fresh start, so to speak. They shave your head, make you wear the exact same clothing as everyone else, and train to you obey commands without hesitation. You lose access many things once taken for granted. Coffee? Nope. Cigarettes? Think again. Books and magazines? Might as well ask to watch TV—but wait! you can't do that either. Also, no internet, no telephone, no music. The whole process is designed to break down your civilian identity to rebuild you as a soldier and member of a team.

Although it royally sucked to endure a four-month experience systematically designed to be unpleasant, it was also liberating. Boot camp had a penitential effect that forced me to reflect on my life up to that point. I found myself ruminating over how I had wronged people in the past, and I meditated on ways to learn from those mistakes. The Anglican confession, as I remembered it from Durham Cathedral often came to mind:

Most merciful God, we confess that we have sinned against you in thought and word and deed, through negligence, through weakness, through our own deliberate fault. We are truly sorry and repent of all our sins.

The process became a form of death and rebirth. Training for war brought questions about God to my awareness that I hadn't considered for years. It's a cliché to say, "there are no atheists in foxholes," but that doesn't make it untrue.

Basic training was often *hilarious*. The strict rules and regulations made every infraction funny. And hierarchy made it even funnier. The more the drill sergeants tried to enforce their standards of behavior on us, the more apt we were to screw them up, which turned each day into a gag reel waiting to happen.

In this world of suspended adolescence and gloriously "toxic" masculinity, marksmanship assumed the same role as other stupid metrics guys use to assess their worth, such as income, IQ, video game score, or bench-press poundage. After each shooting session, each man's most recent score became the new shorthand for his entire value as a person. It was hilarious to watch how the guys who shot well would run around asking everyone else how they scored, while those who shot badly would slink around hangdog, avoiding eye contact. My own scores varied enough that I experienced both the highs and lows of this roller emotional coaster.

One of the most useful life lessons I got from army pop-up target shooting was the principle of *sequential* aiming. In other words, prioritizing, which goes something like this:

As you're lying in the prone (belly on the ground) with your sights downrange and the charging handle jammed up into your helmet, the green plastic targets pop up at random distances during a timed exercise. Some are close at 25 meters, others far away at 300, and others interspersed in between. As these targets pop up, you panic at first, feeling the need to hit them all at once. But then you calm down, realizing you *can't* hit them all at once, and that's the whole point. You've got no choice but to *prioritize*. You aim at the nearest targets first, because they're easiest to hit, and because in real life the nearer enemy would be the more dangerous threat. Once you pick off these easy ones, you shift fire to the harder targets further out. This is a life lesson because it teaches the cardinal virtue of putting things into *proportion*, which often requires you to make choices of what *not* to do.

Cavalry scouts are jacks-of-all-trades. We learned to operate various vehicles and weapons systems, and gained skills in reconnaissance, surveillance, land navigation, hand-to-hand combat, escape and evasion, radio communications, and first aid, to name a few. We learned to move and shoot under fire using three-second rushes, saying to ourselves, "I'm up; he sees me; I'm down." We rehearsed these methods inching across a football field of mulch, helmets and cheeks pressed into the ground as drill sergeants sprayed us with garden hoses.

With the Iraq and Afghanistan wars raging that February in 2005, some of our drill sergeants and cadre were fresh combat veterans from historic units like "Brave Rifles," the Third Cavalry Regiment that helped spearhead the Iraq invasion. As blooded soldiers, they were not cocky in the least. Many seemed shaken and scarred. They treated us with compassion that was sort of scary because it implied what might await us overseas.

The main thing they taught was the need for "force and violence of action." They said that in combat, instantaneous, controlled aggression would determine an outcome more than any other single factor. One of them said, "When facing an enemy or a threat, the moment you decide what to do, do it with *absolute force*. Force and *violence of action* alone can carry a situation before the enemy even knows what happens. And you can't hesitate. Action without hesitation will decide threatening situations before they ever develop."

Of all the ideas described in this book, this brutal recipe for violent action may seem the least gentlemanly if we only think of gentlemen as nice guys who say "please" and "thank you," and who have strong views about Interior decorating. But in the historical context of gentility's roots through the ages, going back to the ancient Greeks, ancient

Israelites, and medieval knights, this aggressive side of the coin is necessary for counterbalancing the aesthetic side. To be in a position to protect the weak, it pays to be as strong as possible: first in general, and then in the small little areas that yield the most return for the least output.

Having said that, I hasten to add that I often felt queasy at basic training when I considered the effects of the weapons we learned to use. Only now, over a decade later, can I admit how anxious I originally felt just to shoot my rifle. The acrid smell of smoke from the receiver made me sick at the thought of shooting another person—or getting shot myself. With time it became an acquired taste, but it never became second nature. Some guys may be naturally tough. Others (like me) can only toughen up through repetitive exposure to hard circumstances.

One of the best lessons I gained from basic training was what we might call "reverse luxury." That is, when you try to increase your pleasures in life by accumulating niceties, luxuries, and comforts, you eventually become "pleasure mad," as my friend's grandmother used to say. When you only care about feeling good, the things that make you feel good can get old after a while, because each time you gain a new pleasurable experience, you adapt to it and start taking it for granted.

By contrast, when you're forced to deal with unpleasant, and even painful things, they reset the bar for what you consider normal. As your "normal" expectations get adjusted downward, you start treating things you once took for granted as happy surprises. Of course, this idea isn't really new; I got it from the ancient Stoics.

After four months of basic training, or "basic hazing" as we Troopers called it, the ordeal finally came to an end. As my buddy John Bansemer said, "Basic training is like pink eye. You have it. It sucks. And then it's over."

Horsemanship

In juxtaposition to Fort Knox, the City Troop opened doors to other activities that fell outside the norm of typical American life. The most vivid of these was learning to ride with the unit's equestrian program.

Our National Guard unit was a cavalry unit. But unlike other cavalry units, we had a dual designation for combat and ceremonial duties. That is, we trained for war and we also trained for mounted horse parades in peacetime. Our riding lessons were held at Valley Forge Military Academy in Wayne, Pennsylvania.

After boot camp, learning to ride horses became the next iteration of my gentleman's education—and it yielded a bumper harvest.

At Valley Forge, we learned basic riding skills like walking, trotting, cantering, and jumping. We also practiced cavalry skills like tent-pegging and snagging rings with a lance while cantering. We also played tag on horseback, which did more to help me develop my "seat," a rider's ability to keep himself grounded to the saddle, than our formal instruction (not that my seat was ever that good). Playing tag reminded me that a playful approach to learning new things often works best.

As John Cleese said in his outstanding talk about creativity, it's helpful to toggle between "open" mode and "closed" mode.[39] *Open mode* allows you to take risks and make mistakes. *Closed mode* is used when you go back with a critical eye and refine what you just learned. Playing tag on horseback reminded me of how, back during my hitch-hiking trip, speaking to strangers and "playing" with the German language was a form of "open mode" learning that accelerated my speaking abilities.

As soldiers, horsemanship supplemented our military training in very special ways. It instilled raw physical courage more than most army stuff did, because horses were more *dangerous* than most army training scenarios. Horses back up unexpectedly and step on your feet, they bite you, and they try to throw you off their backs. Like naughty kids, lazy privates, and indolent college freshmen, they always test you to see what they can get away with.

Because horses are animals of flight, it's essential for riders to be calm, confident, and fearless. They sense a rider's confidence. They can feel how a rider's stomach muscles tighten if he breathes nervously. The instant horses sense fear or hesitancy, they take advantage of it.

As a rider, you have to check horses when they rebel, but you need to gentle enough that they find no reason to rebel. You have to think of their needs, to partner with them as governor and governed. To

---

[39] John Cleese on Creativity in Management, YouTube: https://www.youtube.com/watch?v=Pb5oIIPO62g.

do all this, the first person you have to govern is yourself. Germans call this *Selbstbeherrschung* (self-command). What could be more gentlemanly or ladylike? Try talking with a horsewoman sometime, and you'll be amazed how confident and self-possessed the sport makes her.

Each time you walk into a paddock to fetch your horse, you must behave *very calmly*. Instead of just barging in, you open the gate *slowly*, shut it behind you *softly*. Then you walk past all the other horses *confidently*, because if they sense anything off-beat they'll spook, bite, or kick. When you bridle your horse, he may not want to wear it, so you have to slip it over his head in a polite but firm manner. Again, each body movement requires self-mastery, which (again) makes you a better gentleman.

Speaking of calmness, there are legendary stories of aplomb in riding lore. For example, Regency-era horseman Assheton Smith used to make a point of riding straight into fences no matter how high they were, trusting in the motto: "There's no place you cannot get over with a fall." He'd relax his muscles enough to fall loosely while keeping a firm grip on the reins to avoid the hassle of catching his horse afterward. [40] I've never had the courage to attempt such a method, but it's an admirable concept.

It was fascinating to see how all this stuff cut across gender lines in very traditional ways. A horsey

---

[40] Philip Mason, The English Gentleman: The Rise and Fall of an Ideal (New York: William Morrow & Company, 1982).

Englishwoman quipped, "The best horsewomen come off bitchy and the best horsemen come off gay, because both need to learn skills against their gender types. Women have to harden up, and men have to develop sensitivity and grace that other sports simply don't teach."

Two additional leadership lessons horse riding taught were *situational awareness* and *foresight*.

If you want to stay in the saddle and not get tossed, you must constantly think a few steps ahead of your horse. One woman told me, "You have to make constant adjustments when fox hunting. You must anticipate what's coming and use constant imperceptible adjustments to get the horse there. The adjustments come from the slightest hints and pressure in the hands, seat, and even breathing."

From a military standpoint, these skills translate perfectly for leading men. General Washington was such a compelling leader (and he really, truly was) because he was first an excellent *horseman*.

Horses also teach *clarity*—the need to avoid giving mixed signals. This became apparent one day when a horse tossed me while taking a jump. The instructor pulled me aside afterward and said, "You didn't get thrown off. You merely got bumped off! Why? Because you got nervous right before the jump and pulled back on the reins, asking him to slow up. At the same time, you squeezed him with your heels to ask him to make the jump. You gave

124

two conflicting signals based on your own lack of confidence. And he obeyed! He took the jump, but he also slowed up, and in slowing up, his gait bumped you right out of the saddle. If you learn to take the jumps with full commitment, you'll send one message, not two. The horse will then find his own way over the jump."

What marvelous advice!

With time, I found myself applying all these equestrian principles to human interactions. Walking into an office to see a client, approaching a girl in a cute sundress, or doing foot patrols in Iraq. . . In each case, I learned to slow my breathing, put one foot in front of the other, and imagine I was walking into a paddock.

Volunteering for Iraq

Within a year of returning from basic training, I deployed to Iraq in 2006. A sister unit in our squadron had taken casualties and was looking for unmarried soldiers to volunteer as replacements so those with families wouldn't have to go. Although it scared me to think what this decision could mean, I volunteered for combat duty. I didn't really want to go, but I couldn't *not* go, if that makes any sense.

In retrospect, I was also feeling something Adam Smith described in *Wealth of Nations*:

> The contempt of risk and the presumptuous hope of success, are in no period of life more active than at the age at which young people choose their professions. How little fear of misfortune is then capable of balancing hope of good luck, appears still more evidently in the readiness of the common people to enlist as soldiers, or to go to sea . . . What a common soldier may lose is obvious enough. Without regarding the danger however, young volunteers never enlist so readily as at the beginning of a new war.[41]

After a few months of bureaucratic delay (with which I was perfectly happy), I went to Camp Shelby, Mississippi for training.

---

[41] Adam Smith, *The Wealth of Nations* (New York: Bantam Classics, 2003).

The Mississippi region had just been hit by Hurricane Katrina, which brought down trees and damaged buildings everywhere, but it brought the upside that smashed-up sugar pines filled the woods with a delightful scent. I felt a dull sense of panic upon arrival as I plunged back into army mode so soon after basic training. It was the reverse-luxury cycle all over again—easy to describe in print, but tough to experience in real life.

A crushing sense of loneliness and fear swept over me at first as I met guys in my new unit with whom I would have had little in common in civilian life, but it soon became obvious that everyone was equally afraid. Everyone seemed to realize we were all in the same boat. Fear stripped away people's bravado, which made it easier to make friends.

Of course, it was easy to get annoyed with people, living cheek by jowl around the clock. But whenever someone really irritated me, I realized there were probably lots of ways I irritated them, so I tried to be as agreeable as possible in my own right. This was certainly a lesson in gentlemanly character that I could not have learned any other way.

In other words, *it's easy to be sensitive about things that affect you but insensitive about how you affect others. Far better to reverse things by becoming insensitive to your own feelings, so affronts can slide off you like Teflon.*

Barracks life was a tonic. Durham and Heidelberg had been astonishingly beautiful places with their

127

castles, trees, and rivers, but in a sense, I liked Camp Shelby *more*. I loved the unpainted cinderblock barracks, the raw cement floors, the ancient toilet fixtures streaked with rust, the bare light bulbs screwed into ceiling sockets. The simplicity was immensely calming.

All my possessions fit into a duffel bag. I wore the same clothing every day, carrying the same essential items (wallet, cell phone, Leatherman multitool) in the same exact pockets. Army food at the chow hall was decent, cheap (free), and you never had to clean up afterward. There were no Yvonnes (bless her heart) to complain if you left the toilet seat up. Evenings after training, I would read books with an ear cocked to the hilarious, moronic banter of other guys in the barracks, and would then put in ear plugs to sleep while others were snoring.

At the enlisted men's club, soldiers coming back from Iraq on leave told horror stories about Ramadi (where we were headed), which the media described as the most dangerous place on earth at the time. Wondering about the chance of seeing combat, I sort of *wanted* to experience it. I thought it would give me something in common with people I read about in books. I wanted the chance to exercise Kipling's "If" in real time. But I also knew that such thoughts were naïve. I'd seen movies like *Born on the Fourth of July*, in which the Tom Cruise character volunteers for Vietnam and comes back in a wheelchair. The adult in me (I was twenty-nine

128

years old after all) knew it would be best to see *no action* whatsoever.

The most interesting skill set I acquired while training for Iraq was urban operations, in which we learned how to assault buildings in four-man "stack teams." To do this, you'd line up with three other soldiers outside a door. The three rear soldiers would lean their weight into the guy up front, who would simultaneously lean his weight back against them, which compressed all four guys into a coiled spring. When the door was breached (kicked open), the four-man "spring" would pile into the house all at once, with each man aiming his weapon on a preassigned section of the room.

As wear rehearsed these things, the instructors would insist we do it slowly, without rushing. They'd say, "Slow equals smooth, and smooth equals fast." They'd explain that the best way to perform a complex task quickly is to break it down into its smallest individual parts, rehearse each of these very slowly and very often, and then put them all together into one smooth motion as a masterpiece overall.

Ramadi Province, Iraq

Upon arriving in country, the two most consistent pieces of advice were "stay alert, stay alive," and "pray every time you leave the FOB and every time you get back." My mom and dad were praying too. Dad, a sincere Christian who took the Bible as literally as his Schwenkfeldian (German pietist) ancestors had done for centuries, prayed that I would get back in better shape from Iraq than I was before I left. Such spiritual positivism provided confidence, like the stone ballast on which heavy railroad tracks are laid.

On the day of my first patrol "outside the wire," we formed up at the main gate and stepped off in a staggered column (a tactical walking formation designed to prevent soldiers from bunching too closely together in case of attack), and walked at an easy pace toward the neighboring village. It felt very weird—the first time in my life I ever walked somewhere knowing that people wanted to kill me. (One of our watchtower guards had been shot recently, so we knew there were gunmen in the neighborhood.)

As I took each step and the gravel crunched under my boots, it felt like walking on the moon, and I tried to get my head around the idea that each footstep might possibly be my last. I strained to observe everything around me and found myself seeing the world not as a fluidly moving picture but rather as a series of quick snapshots: *Click, click, click, click.* I've since found that this is a common phenomenon people experience in dangerous situations.

Passages from Psalm 91 suddenly came to mind, which my mom used to read when I had nightmares about rattlesnakes as a child. "You will tread on the lion and the cobra," she would say aloud (I couldn't read yet). "You will trample the great lion and the serpent . . . A thousand may fall at your side, ten thousand at your right hand, but it will not come near you. You will only observe with your eyes and see the punishment of the wicked."[42]

As a five-year-old, I took these passages to mean that God would *literally* protect me from rattlesnakes and warfare. Years later as a college student, I dismissed the Bible as a book worth taking literally, but now on this foot patrol, its explicit meaning suddenly seemed attractive. I suddenly *wanted* Psalm 91 to mean exactly what it said. So, I started praying those verses as a prayer.

As I walked on, heavily outfitted in Kevlar helmet, combat earplugs, ballistic sunglasses, and body armor, with my weapon locked, loaded, and held at the low-ready, I asked myself, "Are the promises in Psalm 91 literal or figurative?" An answer came with lightning speed, filling me with peace from the Holy Spirit, which said, "Yes Drew, Psalm 91 is true, and you can rest in My Word." I continued that patrol—and every other one after it—with a belief in divine providence. Maybe God would keep me from getting hit, maybe he wouldn't, but I would rest in Providence either way. (Later, a less comforting corollary dawned on me: If I could believe the Bible enough to accept the blessings of Psalm 91, I would also have to accept its other promises of eternal reward (both positive and negative) with equal decision.

The Actual Bombshell

Earlier in this book, I described Gisela as a Dutch "bombshell." I used that term figuratively of course, but in Iraq I experienced an *actual* bombshell. This occurred at a time when we were performing daily foot patrols in a dangerous section far away from Camp Blue Diamond in Ramadi province.

Each day, we'd drive out to this region in our 113 armored personnel carriers. We'd park our vehicles in the same spot off the main road and walk through alfalfa fields to a nearby village to perform presence patrols. It was mid-spring by that point, and very beautiful. The sun baked the earth into rock-hard clay. The fields, irrigated by canals, were a strikingly bright green. The sky was deeply blue. Shepherds walked close enough nearby for us to hear bells clanging faintly on the necks of their grazing goats. Every so often, a wild dog would yelp in the distance.

None of us spoke as we moved through these fields, which made the distinctive sounds of foot patrolling especially vivid: thirty pairs of boots striking the ground in broken cadence, weapons and gunmetal clattering, the rustling swish of personal equipment jostling against body armor. It was a good, satisfying, timeless sound, which might well have been familiar to Romans on the march centuries earlier.

Nearly every day, an enemy sniper would shoot at us from some distance away. The barely audible crack of a rifle report would signal the shot. Then a snap in the air or a smack on impact would indicate the incoming bullet. This was most unnerving. But what could you do? Kipling's "If" was utterly worthless for situations like this, but Psalm 91 carried any weight.

The first time I heard the thump of an enemy mortar, we were crossing an open field. A sergeant motioned for everyone to get down, and the mortar round exploded nearby. I was surprised how *underwhelming* it was—just a faint clap followed by a white puff of dust. But the explosion's smallness was deceptive. If one of them landed near you, it could remove your limbs.

As we crouched down under that first mortar strike, I was very afraid, and I suddenly understood why men under fire instinctively want to cluster together. I looked over and saw Ward, a fellow Pennsylvanian. He was young, just out of high school, and he was bracing his head against the same berm as I was. We happened to be facing each other, and it was good to make eye contact, because this was his first time under fire too. We had very little in common as civilians. But he's the only person on earth I've ever made eye contact with during the first mortar strike for both of us.

With time we adjusted to such things, and what once was terrifying became a bit more normal. Over time, the monotony of daily patrols made their danger seem less real. Of all things, ankle sprains now became my biggest concern. On the uneven terrain, I would twist my ankle at the most unexpected and inopportune moments. Walking along, my foot would hit a rock at just the wrong angle and my ankle would buckle beneath my weight. I'd feel the nauseating popping of ligaments and my body would collapse to the ground. This happens to foot soldiers quite often, but you don't read about it much in books.

Eventually these ankle sprains taught me to be slow and cautious when taking steps. Not just physical steps, but figurative ones as well. The ability to calm down and walk slowly is yet another gentleman's lesson I treasure today.

Again, as in Rotterdam, such injuries could have been prevented if I had paid better attention to building raw physical strength. The US Army physical fitness test was aimed at aerobics for office workers. But combat soldiers need sheer physical strength to carry heavy weights (or wounded comrades) and avoid injury. It's appalling to think about in retrospect: I passed the army PT test with flying colors, but couldn't barbell squat my own body weight—barbell squats and deadlifts would have prepared me much better for walking on loose terrain with 70 to 90 pounds of gear.

Then one afternoon, I experienced a real bombshell. Or, more accurately, two 155 mm artillery rounds wired together as a landmine. We were wrapping up another day's boring foot patrol when one of our vehicles hit the IED. Several of us walking in front of the vehicle caught the main shock. It was so *sudden* and so *loud*. You have no idea. My knees buckled beneath me, and then I felt nausea and an impulse to vomit. But I didn't vomit, nor did I urinate or defecate—which are perfectly natural things to do involuntarily when you get shelled. Of course, had my body reacted in any of those ways, there would have been no shame whatsoever.

Stumbling from the blast, for a second, I turned coward and wanted to run away and keep on running for a long time. But a split second later I checked this reaction and threw myself to the ground as we were taught to do at basic training.

Then I stood back up, and a wave of thick smoke washed over me from the stricken vehicle. There were sprinkles of moisture in the smoke, which I took at first to be droplets of blood. The vehicle rolled to a stop with the two guys in it hanging out of the hatches. I braced myself, expecting them to be dead with their torsos beneath the hatches shredded like spaghetti. Happily, however, they weren't spaghetti. They were certainly dazed, but otherwise intact. Also, (thankfully) the droplets of "blood" I thought I felt in the smoke came from someone's Gatorade bottle that had disintegrated in the blast.

To our great good fortune (and a little help from Psalm 91), the vehicle pivoted away from the IED just as it had rolled over it. Had they driven over it directly, the track would have exploded, taking the rest of us with it.

It's very humbling to experience explosions like this, to be shot at by snipers, and to be mortared. It robs you of pride because you realize how a single projectile can kill or cripple you instantly. Since that time, I've received much strength from this vulnerability. It has helped me endure other explosions in life that had nothing to do with war. It has given me an ability to take each day as it comes, with the understanding that each could be my last. It has given depth to my cultivation of the preppy virtues (deference, discretion, modesty, self-restraint, gratitude, and grace) and Kipling's "If."

The Racquet Club of Philadelphia

As spring gave way to summer in Iraq, temperatures climbed above 120 degrees. Our uniforms and body armor (which were comfortable in 50-degree weather back home) became painfully annoying to wear. I wanted so much to whine about how difficult it all felt, but that would have been a major no-no. It astonished me how no one in our platoon ever complained about such things. I guess there was an assumption that complaining would only make it worse. This taught me another crucial gentlemanly lesson: don't whine, suffer silently, and don't complain.

It seemed to take ages, but our deployment finally ended. We cycled home through Kuwait, Mississippi, and finally Pennsylvania. This transition phase was bizarre. At each step, I faced indescribable waves of dislocation unlike anything before or since. To this day, the memory of such loneliness is my chief horror from the war. If such feelings are common to veterans, I understand why suicide rates are so high. It's one thing to absorb new things in the moment (even terrible things), to absorb them as they come, and it's fine to deal with them in retrospect as the dust settles, but there's an awkward middle place between these two poles that can be unbearable.

Iraq was a big test for whether I "believed" in our gentleman's military concept in the First City Troop. When I first joined, I used to wonder, "Is the Troop an army unit with a social club attached to it, or a social club with military pretensions?" Iraq taught me that it was *both*—and much, much more. The very things that made the Troop seem silly from a professional military perspective and absurd from a civilian viewpoint made it magnificent for long-term community. Indeed, many civilians and veterans languish equally in life because they lack the sort of comradery the First City Troop provides. I wish every city had more organizations of its type.

Upon returning home to Pennsylvania, I noticed some quirks and bizarre tics left over from Iraq. For a while, I couldn't go anywhere without constantly scanning my surroundings. I was always on the lookout for things that "didn't look right." I found myself instinctively bracing for explosions, sniper bullets, or other unexpected attacks. While walking down Philadelphia streets, I would scan rooftops, keeping an eye out for places to take cover, and pause before stepping around corners with the same sense of alertness from prior weeks in Iraq. This stuff didn't feel like paranoia, but more like a sense of "warrior craftsmanship."

It was very, very bizarre to revisit the Racquet Club of Philadelphia (affectionately known as the "RCOP"), a beautifully appointed building near Rittenhouse Square designed by Horace Trumbauer. Junior Troopers were often members and would go there after final formation on drill weekends to partake in the "tribathalon," a three-part event which included sitting in steam room, sitting in the sauna, and diving into the swimming pool.

RCOP hosted Wednesday cocktail parties each summer which attracted prospective members, Penn students, and other locals. We had often gone to these before the deployment. And now it was very strange to see my fellow Troopers there, fresh from Ramadi, smartly dressed in summer blazers and bow ties, standing rigidly among all the people who seemed unchanged from the year before. You could instantly identify the Ramadi Troopers because their faces were drawn and gaunt around the cheekbones and eye sockets.

For a while, it was hard for me to take anyone seriously who had not been to war, especially guys my own age. Cocky civilian dudes suddenly seemed laughable. The more confident any jackass seemed to be about his looks, charms, smarts, strength, career, wealth, or whatever other edge he thought he had on life, the more I felt like I could walk right through him. It's not that I felt special in comparison to them, it's that I appreciated how fleeting things are, and how no one's talents or abilities can withstand' a well-placed bombshell.

Meschter Insurance

After Iraq, my father offered me a job at Meschter Insurance, our family business. Small businesses are funny. In some families they can seem like living organisms or invisible guests at the dinner table every night. When I was a kid, Dad was never one for tossing the football or going fishing, but business was something we could always talk about.

Business is an interesting subject from the standpoint of this whole *gentleman* thing. In Britain, commerce traditionally disqualified one from being considered a gentleman. For-profit trade was looked down on and "disinterested" occupations were preferred in the church, military, and professions. But America has always been different. Our first colonies were founded as joint-stock trading companies. And we have always had a strain of thought, rooted in Jeffersonian Democracy which values small-scale businesses in which citizens are forced to make hard, independent decisions as owner-operators. With all this in mind fresh from Iraq, I treated insurance as a noble enterprise. For inspiration I read corporate histories of firms like Philadelphia Contributionship, State Farm, Insurance Company of North America, and Lloyds of London, getting a feel for industry lore.

It would be hard to imagine anything more unlike the army than our seven-person mom-and-pop office in exurban Collegeville, Pennsylvania with its corporate culture modeled on Harleysville Savings, a local Mennonite bank with which my dad was also involved.

Dad's dad started the agency back in 1953 when he bought a shoebox full of index cards from old Kep Tyson, the local insurance man in Skippack Village whose lawn my grandfather mowed as a boy. In an act of considerable bravery, my grandparents traded their life savings for Tyson's index cards which carried the name and policy details for each client.[43] They went home and dumped the box on the floor, spreading out the cards to figure out who was who. Pop Pop started calling the people, Mom Mom got to work on a typewriter, and they worked as partners from then on. By the time I came along, the firm was like Jimmy Stewart's Bedford Falls Building and Loan in the Christmas movie *It's a Wonderful Life*.

On my first day at work, Dad greeted me with a broadside of do's and don'ts ending with "*And don't park your car in anyone else's spot.*" Without missing a beat, he said, "One more thing!" and handed me a full trash bag to take out to the dumpster. Which is exactly what his dad did on my dad's first day at the office back in 1974.

---

[43] Corporate continuity is an interesting thing. Tyson probably bought his own box of index cards from the local agent back in the 1920s, who probably bought them from someone else a generation earlier. The original business may date from the 1870s, changing with time like the old woodsman's axe that went through five handles and three axe heads in fifty years.

Training for Egypt

Within months of taking out the garbage for Dad however, the First City Troop got deployed to Egypt for a whole year, and I had no choice but to accompany them. Breaking this news to my "boss" who just paid for my insurance training was *decidedly* unpleasant. But he recovered.

Troopers were clucking like hens about this upcoming deployment, trading gossip in what we jokingly called "the sewing circle." When my buddy Brandon and I discussed these things in the Troop's NCO Club, he slammed his ham-like fist on the bar and said, "I don't wanna to go to Egypt! I want combat duty in Afghanistan!"

Poor Brandon. By any reckoning, getting sent to the Sinai Peninsula for Israeli-Egyptian peacekeeping operations with the Multinational Force and Observers (MFO) was a plum assignment in 2007, when the Iraq and Afghanistan conflicts were still raging. But Brandon was upset because he wanted to test himself in combat. I clapped him on the back and said, "Brandon, you don't *really* want to go Afghanistan, do you? It's the graveyard of empires!" He sighed and said, "Aw man, I know I don't *really* want to go to Afghanistan. But I want to *have already been* there, so then *I* can be the guy at the bar who gets to say, *Son, you don't really want to go to Afghanistan.*"

At that we burst out laughing, because what he said was so true. Afghanistan was the challenge Brandon *thought* he wanted. But we both knew Egypt was preferable. And I reminded Brandon that by joining the army when he did after 9/11, he already qualified as a "citizen" in our ancient Athenian/Roman Republican sense. This rationale seemed to comfort him greatly.

Like other young bucks in the Troop, Brandon wasn't your average US Army private. He'd been to a good prep school (Haverford) and then studied at the University of Pennsylvania after *rejecting* Harvard in hope of going to the Naval Academy. His mom put her foot down about Annapolis, saying, "No son of mine is ever joining the military!" So as soon as he finished college, Brandon joined the Troop.

Army logic dictated that to train for the desert, we should first fly across the continent in the *opposite* direction from Egypt to spend a month the rain forest at Fort Lewis in the Pacific Northwest. When our buses reached Lewis, one of the army's largest and best equipped full-time posts, we were amazed how new the buildings were in comparison with our aging World War II barracks back home. But just as our busses slowed down in front of these palaces to suggest we'd be staying there, they turned down a road that got progressively worse the farther we drove, until it finally ended at a group of decrepit wooden structures dating from World War II.

Serving in the National Guard brings rewards great and small, but the transition from civilian life to "army mode" wasn't one of them. What made the transition so painful was how each successive layer of high command clamped down on discipline to remind *themselves* to buckle down, which forced every layer beneath them to tighten up even more. By the time this process reached us lower enlisted men, we were hit with an avalanche of restrictions making life feel just like a jail sentence, or basic training, which is pretty much the same thing. We all agreed that the movie best echoing our lives was the prison film *Shawshank Redemption*.

Of course, First City Troopers have been dealing with this phenomenon for generations. As one Civil War veteran wrote, "The rigid discipline of the camp is rather hard upon a man who has always been free to go as he pleases and the discipline in the Troop camp was always as strict as that of the regulars. With gentlemen it was only necessary to notice quietly any little infraction of duty, and no punishments were ever inflicted."[44]

Chafing against army mode, we made a point of allowing our idiosyncrasies to flourish. Josh West drew titters when he purchased custom tanker boots from Dehner and a russet-colored bridle-leather pistol holster. Tyler Hathaway won infamy at the squadron mail office (and accolades in the Troop) by filling out forms in blue ink with a Mont Blanc

---

[44] *History of the First Troop Philadelphia City Cavalry*, (Philadelphia: Hallowell & Company, 1874).

fountain pen. (This was a double infraction against cultural norms, as it was considered un-military to use anything but black ballpoint.) Brandon Adams formed weekly "Junto" meetings on Benjamin Franklin's model, and recited poems aloud at mealtimes from an anthology. (He received from raised eyebrows from this, but he was physically menacing enough to avoid further comment.) Other Troopers spent free time practicing with flyrods or playing croquet. We all dressed in "Troop casual" when possible: blazers and neckties for special dinners, chinos and pastel shirts, and other gear not popular among normal soldiers.

It was nice spend so much time with certain people, but very annoying to be among others. This triggered a new character-building process for becoming a better gentleman. It occurred to me that whenever people bothered me, I should use them as a *tool* for becoming less offensive myself. I decided that instead of getting angry at such people, I would judo flip offenders into becoming my *teachers*. I'd study their bad traits in order to remove similar ones from myself, and I'd study their good traits in order to adopt them.

As an Honorary Troop Captain once said, the greatest service some people can provide is to be "contraindicators." You observe what they think, say, and do—and then do the exact *opposite*.

Amazingly, I quickly found that some people who bothered me most became my best teachers, and eventually they became great friends. Other people remained annoying, but it was fun to watch them shipwreck as others jumped on their traits which bothered me most. It reminded me of all those instances in the Bible when God would defeat Israel's enemies by turning them against each other, leaving Israel free to pick up the plunder.

Promotion to Sergeant

Around that time the Troop elected a new captain, Anselm Richards, who had recently led a cavalry platoon in Iraq. Having seen combat in Ramadi, he sought to transform the Troop from its cold-war fun-and-games emphasis to a modern war footing. But this was no easy task. Many wondered if we could survive the transition.

Captain Richards was a handsome, tallish, squarely built man, with a senatorial appearance and superb command presence. He had a sharp sense of humor and could obliterate anyone who gave him trouble. One quip from Richards made you feel like that Australian crocodile man who got stabbed in the heart by a stingray.

Upon returning from Iraq, I really wanted to become an officer, which had been a dream since youth. But Troop custom demanded I wait to be "tapped" for it, as if waiting to pledge a college society. Since colonial times, it was considered bad form for "fighting Quakers" to express any interest in promotion, just as the Founding Fathers used to make a point of not wanting to appear as if they wanted to seek political office. Moreover, it was considered just as honorable to be Troop private as Troop commander.

Some older Troop officers told me I should go to Officer Candidate School. But when I brought the matter up with Captain Richards, he nixed it saying,

"The Troop needs NCOs [noncommissioned officers] right now more than it needs officers." I protested his answer vociferously, peevishly, and quite disrespectfully, but ultimately the Troop came first, and I had no choice but to comply. It was a boo-hoo personal tragedy for a while, but service is service. Within weeks I got the consolation prize of promotion to sergeant. Upon giving me the new rank insignia, Captain Richards snapped a figurative towel at me and said, "Christmas came early for you Meschter."

Passing from the rank of Specialist (a glorified private) to Sergeant is a quantum leap in the US Army. It's like getting your driver's license. It's the first time you're a "citizen" so to speak. It's when higher ranking soldiers suddenly stop treating you as if you're in diapers.

An E5 (sergeant) oversees three soldiers in a four-man fire team, the smallest unit configuration in the military. To my surprise, bridging the gap from specialist to sergeant was among the greatest challenges I've ever faced. Newly minted E5s deal with lots of jealousy from former peers who wish *they* had been promoted. In response to this reaction, brand-new sergeants often *overcompensate* by acting much bossier than necessary, ever ready to interpret familiarity from their old comrades as an affront.

In my opinion, overcompensation in any form is the least gentlemanly trait imaginable. It's the ultimate indication that you're trying to display something externally that you lack internally. But some situations are so dashed awkward it's impossible not to overcompensate while you're struggling to get your bearings. In other words, overcompensation is an ugly but necessary part of any learning curve.

Happily, just as manners provide gentlemen with a playbook for social situations, each military rank comes with its own "script" of canned theatrics you can put on like a garment. I've never met a soldier who didn't acknowledge this. Such playacting is not considered inauthentic, but rather shrewd. It's a matter of "Fake it till you make it."

Like a colt taking its first steps, I felt so uncertain and yet so compelled to *seem* certain that I bristled at any sign of disrespect from the guys on my new team. But you can't demand respect; you can only earn it. Combat units demand brusque confrontational interactions with short, sharp phrasing that would be totally inappropriate in civilian life. But confrontation is militarily "polite," so to speak, because decisiveness saves lives. As I found my footing, success eventually came in zigs and zags like a Wall Street stock trending into a bull run. There were advances, retreats, momentary spikes and harrowing plummets, but over time my learning curve moved on the uptick.

One day a capable sergeant from Northeast Philly pulled me aside and said, "Meschter, you're a curious guy; you always ask people questions. But for kids who grew up in tough neighborhoods, *asking questions displays weakness*. They'd rather pretend they already know things even if they don't have a clue. They act cool. You never see me asking anything. I just observe and pick things up by watching. Try doing that for a change. Just keep quiet, pretend you already know all about whatever's going on, and pretend you don't care." This advice ran counter to everything life had ever taught me. But I tried it—and noticed immediate results.

Another NCO lesson was learning to speak to people in *declarative* sentences. Being a sergeant forced me to learn what British literature once called "the habit of command." Which basically means knowing how to boss people around in such a way that they don't resent it. This is *truly* an art form, learned through trial and error in group environments that condone such bluster. It's a matter of applying just the right amount of force at just the right moments in just the right places.

In my experience, this only works if you yourself are under someone else's command. This allows you to put pressure on others while letting them know that you're receiving similar pressure from above. American soldiers are egalitarians even in uniform, and they are experts at knowing what they can get away with authority-wise. They didn't invent the term "barracks lawyer" for nothing.

Tiran Island

Once we finished our miserable train-up at Fort Lewis, we flew back across the United States (*toward* Egypt this time), stopping for layovers in Mississippi, Maine, and Germany along the way.

Upon arriving in Sharm el Sheikh, we were delighted by the physical setting. Our military post (called South Camp) was simply stunning. Set on the Red Sea, it faced the Gulf of Aqaba with majestic Tiran Island in the distance. Behind the camp were jagged mountains that cycled through various shades of dark brown, light brown, pink, and purple as the sun rose and fell. The sea was a dark navy blue with heavy swells and whitecaps driven by winter gusts that would blow off your hat unless you tilted your face down at just the right angle. Down the hill was even a *beach* where people could swim when the weather got better. From "Joe's" perspective (Joe is the nickname given to all American soldiers) this place was a fantasy land.

While we instantly fell in love with these surroundings, within weeks everyone—Joes being who they are—everyone found things to complain about. It's strange how quickly you can adapt to the most beautiful places on one hand, and how numb you can grow to squalor on the other. Iraq, Durham, and Heidelberg had taught me to enjoy both extremes for different reasons.

As we sat down to breakfast that first morning at window facing the Red Sea, where refracted sunlight turned everyone's water glass into prisms, Sergeant Wrabley set down his tray, pointed out the window and said, "See that island out there? We're flying there tomorrow! And we're staying there for the next three weeks." This was stupendous news. Everyone had been wondering which unit would get assigned to the island and every unit was hoping it would be them.

The next day, we crossed the Strait of Tiran in Blackhawk helicopters, watching the choppy sea (filled with sharks) beneath us. Upon our landing, the squad we were replacing from the Puerto Rican National Guard gave us a tour of the place. The island's observation post, officially called OP 3-11, was a tiny affair with several trailers surrounded by earthen HESCO barriers. Two flea-ridden golden retrievers lived full time on post as "guard" dogs. Our ten-man squad slept in a single narrow bunkhouse. They told us to watch our step when walking around outside the area, because Tiran had been a major strategic point during the last Israeli-Egyptian war, and was said to have as many landmines as anywhere on earth.

We used a crude latrine outside and burned its refuse each week with gasoline. Weekly "shit-burning detail" as we loftily called it, was something to behold. The guys put on gas masks and, feeding off each other's energy, made the whole thing into a much bigger deal than it needed to be. Their antics

153

were uproariously funny, especially since I got to watch from a safe directive distance.

Life on the island was laid back, like a Jimmy Buffett song. Our sole mission was to watch the skies and seaways to report any military or naval vehicles in sight. We'd been trained to identify a range of planes, ships, and land craft from all nations operating in that zone. Aside from that, there wasn't much else to do aside from daily housekeeping, watching movies, and eating ice cream.

I'd always wondered what it would be like to spend time in one of those low-security prisons where you can lift weights and study for a law degree, and this turned out to be just such an opportunity. Our guys manned the watchtower in shifts while Sergeant Mullen and I kept an ear on a radio in the Tactical Operations Center (TOC). This left plenty of time for devouring books from amazon and working out. As an omnivorous reader, Sergeant Wrabley was equally pleased with the situation himself.

We couldn't have asked for a better squad leader than Bill Wrabley. A lawyer by profession, he had a sharp Jesuit intellect. He had once been a finance officer in the air force and retained the Fortune 500 management style native to that branch of service. He was smooth as silk to deal with.

In addition to reading books, watching movies, and doing occasional hikes to explore the island like Swiss Family Robinson, we performed routine battle drills to rehearse how to react in case of attack. Sergeant Wrabley made each of us draw sector maps for the machine-gun positions on post to familiarize us with their lines of fire. To estimate distances, he stood on each pillbox and hit golf balls. When we ribbed him for this, he said, "I know exactly how far I hit with my driver, so it's more accurate than walking up those hills, which might give us the wrong distance by foot count." The biggest danger on post were the scorpions and sand vipers that occasionally found their way into the pill boxes.

The day we arrived on Tiran, the out-going squad leader warned that our most difficult task on the island would be managing the weekly helicopter visits bringing food, fuel, and water from South Camp. The helicopters would bring our water supply each week in massive rubber barrels called blivets. As each blivet load arrived, we would have to pump the contents into a water tank. The water pump was notoriously finicky and wouldn't cooperate unless you adjusted the valve *just* right.

Our superiors told Sergeant Wrabley that if we couldn't master this water blivet operation, we'd lose our chance to stay on the island. Many other squads had been booted off over the years for messing it up, and other squads were now hoping we would mess up, so they could get a chance to live there.

When our first re-supply day took place, it didn't go smoothly. Expert army pilots flew in with heavy sling load cargo nets hung under each helicopter. Because wind conditions on the island were normally severe, with gusts hitting the mountainsides from the sea and rushing violently upward, it was very tricky for even the most expert pilots to hover and land. Each time a helicopter came in for a sling-load drop, some of us had to stand directly underneath and hook a grounding wire to its belly to prevent static electric shock when it landed. This job became adventurous, because the Blackhawks kicked up a maelstrom of rocks and sand whenever they landed. Two guys would often have to stabilize whoever held the grounding wire.

With all this stuff going on, it was easy to mess up. When we handled the water blivets the first time, we failed miserably. The pump wouldn't connect with the valve on each blivet, the water wouldn't off-load, and the helicopters had to waste time and fuel hovering overhead. Ashamed of this failure, Sergeant Wrabley assembled us together that evening to perform a magical exercise known throughout the US military as an after-action review (AAR).

An AAR is like an *autopsy* that allows you to dissect any operation to improve it. It hinges on gathering the input from everyone involved, regardless of rank. It's the most democratic practice imaginable. As a free-for-all, everyone brainstorms ideas, and lower ranking people get a chance to criticize superiors. They debate and assess what went right and what went wrong, and no one can hang back without saying anything. Shy people have to speak up. Talkers must yield the proverbial *Lord of the Flies* "conch shell" to others for a change. Nothing could be healthier.

The real "magic" comes when each man sums up his thoughts by naming three things to "sustain" for next time and three things to "improve." That's "three *ups*" and "three *downs*" from each soldier. Because the analysis is always 50 percent positive and 50 percent negative, and because it draws on everyone's viewpoint regardless of rank, it produces balanced innovations.

Through this particular AAR, we reverse engineered the water-blivet process and realized that our lowest-ranking man, Private DeJesus (a dishwasher by trade back home) exhibited special talent in massaging the water pump valve. So, Sergeant Wrabley decided to have him focus exclusively on that task to the exclusion of all else. And since the water valve was the lynchpin for the entire operation, we decided to put DeJesus in command of our *entire* squad during the water blivet downloads. We then revamped the off-loading process entirely around him, mapping out how to bring the blivets up to him on one side of the pump and take the empty ones away from the other.

Thus, thanks to an AAR compiled by nine privates, two buck sergeants, and Staff Sergeant Wrabley, our lowest-ranking man became the most important guy in the most important operation that dictated whether we could remain on the island.

The next week we faced the incoming water supply with fresh eagerness to try our new system. The first wave of Blackhawks came in, and DeJesus assumed an air of tremendous gravity. As each blivet shipment landed, we rolled the barrels up to him, he hooked them to the pump, and then used his savant-like feel for water flow to finesse the valve. I'll never forget the joy of watching him rise to the occasion that Sunday, how his expression hardened with concentration as the helicopters arrived, and how he stepped up to his role as *maestro*.

From that day on, water shipments were a breeze. Each week, DeJesus would become a hero for three hours, and each week after the water-blivet operation ended, he would go back to being his normal unassuming self without missing a beat.

Thanks to our success with these water blivets, Captain Richards assigned us to Tiran Island each monthly cycle for the rest of the year. This tremendous good fortune saved us from manning less attractive posts in the region, such as "Fly Ville," the nickname for a miserable hovel situated in an airless gully next to a garbage dump where impoverished Bedouin kids stirred up flies while picking through trash for rotten scraps of food.

Although I joined the National Guard with an aim to face some of the character-building challenges that captured my imagination about the Victorian public schools, the army was now teaching me leadership lessons I couldn't have acquired anywhere else. Sure, Wharton or Harvard Business School might have taught me lots of things about working in big organizations, but nothing could have taught what the army did about small-team operations in the enlisted ranks. This view was not uncommon among First City Troopers. As one Trooper said, "Back in the 1970s, the National Guard taught me ten times more about leadership than anything I ever got from Wharton Business School."

Dawn Patrols from North Camp

After a few months in Egypt, "Bill Czernin" joined our squad. That's not his real name by a long shot, but the pseudonym he wanted for this book. He was twenty-one years old (ten years my junior) and still in college. He grew up in northern Pennsylvania on a big wooded property overlooking the Delaware Water Gap.

Like Brandon and I, "Bill" believed in the citizen-soldier concept as described by Alexis de Tocqueville in *Democracy in America*. And like many Troopers, he grew up on easy terms with people in authority. This made it very hard for him to take orders from people who didn't also ask for his advice. Learning to submit to authority was therefore tough for him, but a very good character builder. Submission taught him the gentlemanly virtue of *deference*.

He joined our squad just in time for a new mission to North Camp, our post in northern Sinai on the Egyptian-Israeli border. At North Camp, our job was to wake up each morning at four thirty and drive up-armored Humvees on patrols to secure the routes leading to and from camp. These drives took us through Bedouin villages and miles of desert to the Israeli border. The Bedouin villages were "hostile" to the extent that kids threw rocks at us. The desert stretches, were glorious with color variations of browns, whites, and pinks changing tone as the sun rose.

These daily drives often felt like road trips and provided an ideal venue for running conversations about anything and everything. In free-ranging chats, we shouted ourselves hoarse over the roaring engines, solving the world's problems, hashing out observations about the Troop, life, women, Pennsylvania, geopolitics—you name it.

Life at the bottom of the military totem pole made Bill think a lot about matters of hierarchy and leadership. When he was at basic training, a drill sergeant named Seabring took him under his wing and gave words of advice that stayed with Bill forever.

Sergeant Seabring was typical of the sort of gem you can find in the US military. A crafty, hyper-intelligent go-getter who worked his way up from humble beginnings, he enlisted in the US Marines after high school, switched to the National Guard, and then worked his way through college by day-trading stocks while sleeping in his car. After a decade or so living rough in combat units, he was full of wise counsel about life in large military bureaucracies.

Among Seabring's maxims was the idea that you need to counterbalance by-the-book training with fresh innovation. He said, "Study all the field manuals front to back until you know them cold. Eighty percent of success in the military comes from memorizing your lines before everyone else does. Then once you master all that domain knowledge, you can experiment with new methods as you see fit." In other words, instead of rebelling against the "system," feeling you're some kind of inspirational genius who is above "doing things by the book," you should learn the book before trying to rewrite it.

This concept convicted me because I'd always rebelled against standard operating procedures (SOPs), preferring to do my own thing on the fly, which is why I was so infatuated with "the British genius for improvisation" concept of throwing yourself into unknown circumstances and muddling through. But it dawned on me that you can only improve a system after you first get a chance to understand its moving parts. And you can't know the moving parts until you learn (and even memorize) its SOPs.

This led to a new lesson: a gentleman should first be able to *obey* the rules of a system before he can attempt to *innovate* them.

Seabring boiled leadership down into "Three C's" that are worth exploring in detail:

> Competence
> Candor
> Consistency

Competence was the most important trait, and pretty much self-explanatory. In the vernacular we could say, "To be competent, you must know your shit cold." In other words, to be competent, you *can't*

162

fake it till you make it, because fakeness on your part will be found out, and everyone will suffer.

Candor is essential because it eliminates the rumors and guessing games that occur in any organization when lower-ranking people don't know what the higher-ups are doing. Weak leaders often get stingy with information because they think "information is power." But people are smart enough to know when they're not getting the full picture. They'll wind up forming an image based on rumor and speculation that may well become poisonous. By contrast, candor builds trust. Bill and I stewed about this a lot because we thought candor was the virtue most lacking in our own leaders at the time.

Consistency came last but not least. Seabring believed that subordinates psychologically need to be able to *predict* a superior's reaction to things, the way we can all predict when the sun comes up each day. He said, "Soldiers can adjust to almost *anything* their leaders dish out. But even a lab rat needs to know which door leads to cheese and which brings an electric shock. You can't go switching doors around on the poor guy."

Inspired by Seabring, Bill and I raved about how many brilliant people there were in the military who had never gone to college, and who honed a different sort of intelligence in the ranks. Their basket of abilities included situational awareness, bureaucratic slyness, emotional empathy, verbal acuity, and pragmatic learning by doing, to name but a few. We were always amazed at how bright American enlisted men could be and how moronic our officers could be. Of course, we always admitted that if we had become officers straight from college, we'd be just as bad, and probably worse.

Greasing the Groove

While military service taught me social and intellectual lessons that aided my development as a citizen and all-rounder, it also brought physical lessons no less vital. The mind-body connection has always been a crucial part of the gentlemanly ideal: "mens sana in corpore sano" (a healthy mind in a healthy body).

As indicated above, for years I struggled with finding the right physical fitness program for building the sort of body I needed to be a man of both thought and action. Some of the mishaps I experienced over the years (the bicycle failure in Rotterdam, ankle sprains in Iraq, a knee dislocation while ice skating) came from not having enough leg strength. I eventually learned that strength is the best form of injury protection. But how to go about building it?

One role model in this quest was Teddy Roosevelt. As a kid, he was bright but frightfully asthmatic and scrawny. One day his father pulled him aside and said, "Theodore, you have the mind, but you have not the body, and without the help of the body the mind cannot go as far as it should. You must make your body. It is hard drudgery to make one's body, but I know you will do it."[45]

---

[45] Edmund Morris, *The Rise of Theodore Roosevelt* (New York: Random House Trade Paperbacks, 2001) .

Roosevelt accepted this challenge and spent hours in a home gymnasium grinding away on parallel bars and pulley apparatus. His sisters were astonished at his diligence, but when "Teedy" went on vacation that summer in Maine, two local boys gave him trouble and he was too weak to fight back. Reminiscing he said, "The worst feature was that when I finally tried to fight them, I discovered that either one singly could not only handle me with easy contempt but handle me so as not to hurt me much and yet prevent my doing any damage whatever in return."[46] Upon returning home, Roosevelt redoubled his efforts and eventually built himself into a man who could take a beating—and return it.

This example fascinated me when I first read about it in high school, and for years I found ways to emulate it. Time and again, I threw myself into challenging situations, usually underperformed, and then limped back to the drawing board.

In school I swam and played water polo, but those activities never built any real strength. In college I tried to remedy this by lifting weights (with little progress) and working summer jobs in masonry and heavy landscaping. The masonry job taught me that you can lift a lot more weight than you think by simply saying the word "UP!" to yourself as you hoist it off the ground. I also learned that among working guys who don't care a damn how you feel, you yourself don't feel as much pain when you get

---

[46] Edmund Morris, *The Rise of Theodore Roosevelt* (New York: Random House Trade Paperbacks, 2001).

injured. And I learned that if you face off with an angry drunken bricklayer twice your size, not caring if he hits you, he just might back down and throw you a backhanded compliment for standing up to him. On other occasions I worked on a historic tall ship and moved furniture at an auction house, which provided much better training for lifting heavy objects and hoisting heavy lines.

It all came together when my friend Mark introduced me to some books and videos by Pavel Tsatsouline, a Russian fitness instructor who introduced kettlebell training to America. Pavel wrote an article called "Grease the Groove for Strength"[47] that finally set me on the right path to building functional fitness.

According to Pavel, to get good at anything, you must do it *often*, and to the exclusion of other things. He used the equation *specificity + frequent practice = success.* His approach required no pain endurance whatsoever. He insisted that you should never train to failure; "you should work as strong as you can while staying as fresh as you can," which reminded me of the urban operations mantra "slow equals smooth, and smooth equals slow." This seemed like the perfect gentleman's approach to working hard while hardly working.

---

[47] Pavel Tsatsouline, "Grease the Groove for Strength," *MILO: A Journal for Serious Strength Athletes* (1999). Copies of the article are also available online.

Using Pavel's method, I managed to get stronger and more functionally fit in my thirties (and now in my forties) than I ever was in my twenties. It all paid off one summer at the beach when a girlfriend said, "You look like someone who could handle himself in a bar fight." She'd never seen a barfight in her life, but I was happy with the comment.

As a team leader in Egypt, I had the chance to try Pavel's process on my own test monkeys: the guys in my team. They came from noncombat units (fuelers, truck drivers, and administrative personnel) that deemphasized the need for physical training. All three national guardsmen had trouble passing the Army Physical Fitness Test (APFT). They were weak, overweight, and disinterested in fitness. They excelled at video games of course, but that wouldn't do us any good if they had to carry a wounded man.

Sergeant Wrabley and I talked about how to get them in shape. He focused on the whole squad, while I focused on my three guys. Instead of forcing them to work hard ("no pain, no gain"), which would only make them dread working out, I used Pavel's gentlemanly approach of gain without pain. I promised them they'd rarely have to work beyond their comfort level. They could work at *half* their capacity as long as they doubled their volume.

For example, if they could do twenty pushups, I'd ask them to do three sets of ten. If they could jog a mile, I'd only ask them to jog half a mile, but to do it every day before dinner while staying in their comfort zones. If we all did a group run, I'd trot behind the slowest guy so he wouldn't feel like he was bringing up the rear. By dialing things back to their comfort zone, they eventually *expanded* their comfort zones, and *fitness overtook them.*

The main thing was getting them to disassociate exercise with that panicky feeling you get when forced to work beyond your ability. By creating a sense of ease and accomplishment, they started to enjoy the feeling of success. With time, they started going out for runs on their own and doing pushups on their own. They started flexing in the mirror and liking what they saw.

This tied into the gentlemanly ideal because it was a fitness method that emphasized a "light touch" to get people to want to do things that were in their best interest anyway, while keeping strict parameters to stay on target.

The Way Up Is Down

Although our year in the Sinai had lots of high points, it also ground us down in various ways. Not all our assignments were as pleasant as Tran Island and North Camp. We also spent weeks doing monotonous gate guard at South Camp for hours on end looking into nothing, alternating day-and-night shifts that played havoc with circadian rhythms. "Free time" was filled with make-work projects to keep Joe busy, making it very hard to find time for swimming at South Camp's tantalizing beach.

All this stuff brought us together as friends and even *brothers*. But comradery came with a cost. As young Bill Czernin said, "Egypt was a pressure cooker. Nothing specifically military about the experience affected me at all, but the constant abrasion with other people brought me to a slight breaking point every day."

Forced proximity in our squads all year indeed had a pressure-cooker effect on everyone involved. We chafed at each other's flaws and told each other what we thought of them—sometimes kindly, but more often by blowing up. There were many cycles of iron sharpening iron, and many resulting sparks.

Back when I first discovered the Troop in 2003, Andy Sullivan said, "The guys in this unit will eventually become your best friends." Upon hearing him say that, I thought he was full of crap. I thought,

"How on earth can you predict who will become your best friends?"

But Egypt taught me that Sullivan was right. Special relationships form when people are forced together with no option to bail out. In such "covenant" relationships, you pledge yourself to others as a form of social contract that transcends momentary feelings, which permits genuine affection eventually follow. An army line unit forces you into a platonic marriage with no options for divorce.

It's one thing to spend "quality time" with people when you're feeling good and you can always present your best fake self, as people do constantly on social media, but the National Guard forced us to spend "quantity time" together when we didn't want to be there. (The word *comrade* stems from a Latin root meaning "to share the same room.") Most of the time in uniform was "downtime," absolutely wasted time that you'd never voluntarily spend if you had the choice. But that is precisely what built strong friendships.

Paradoxically, *quantity time* when nothing of interest seems to be happening is what provides the opportunity for spontaneous *quality* interactions to pop up that could never occur otherwise. It provides a context for both good and bad things to bubble up that would have remained hidden for years under normal circumstances.

Normal life allows you to provide a packaged version of yourself to the world. Often this is unavoidable and even preferable. But the First City Troop, with its Philadelphian emphasis on being comfortable in who you are, tended to remove such packaging. While the Troop provided plenty of opportunities for members to buff up their polish in a dazzling array of social settings, its greatest benefit was the way it roughed us up as well.

Bill and I struggled with this until we found a golden key through a sermon by Derek Prince. Prince was an interesting Christian teacher, seemingly custom made for us who was born in India, educated at Eton, became a logic professor at Cambridge, and served as a medic in Montgomery's Eighth Army in World War II. Later in life he became a Pentecostal preacher, which for those familiar with both Oxbridge and that denomination, is an astounding conversion. Bill and I discovered his radio talks on the internet while we were in Egypt, and we listened to them avidly.

Prince's most powerful talk was called "The Way Up Is Down"[48] in which he explored Jesus's statement, "Whoever exalts himself will be humbled, and he who humbles himself will be exalted."[49] His idea was that if you try to exalt yourself in life, others will resent and resist you, and God will ultimately humble you. But if you put others above yourself,

---

[48] Derek Prince, "The Way Up Is Down," sermon, https://www.derekprince.org/.
[49] Matt. 23:12 NKJV.

God will exalt you and others will follow suit.[50] Prince made a memorable correlation between pride and the law of gravity: *In physics, what goes up must come down; in matters of human ego, what goes down must come up.*

Bill and I found this fascinating. We tried field testing it with people and discovered amazing results. We started making a point of putting others above ourselves and adopted a new rule:

> *Always assume that maybe you are 49 percent correct and the person who bothers you is 51 percent correct.*

This provided a ratio for giving others the benefit of the doubt and leaving room to learn from them even when they are wrong. It's a concept that has revolutionized my life ever since. Once Bill and I started placing others first, using the 49% - 51% rule, doors opened with people that never would have opened otherwise.

After years of trying to become a better man, and a thoroughgoing gentleman, this lesson finally put me over the top. It's the silver bullet that finally made me feel comfortable in my own skin. Thinking back on life, I was a *mess* at age thirteen, even *more* of a mess at age twenty-three, but by thirty-three I finally felt like a going concern.

---

[50] A corollary is the idea, "He who would be first must be last, and he who would be a ruler must be a slave." Mark 10:43.

Fast forward to January 2018, when I sat down at a coffee shop one day in Philadelphia to work on this book. I got a good table La Colombe off Rittenhouse Square. The weather was cold outside but bright and sunny. The floors were salty from people tracking in slush. A clean-cut looking guy sat down at the table next to me and started reading Ron Chernow's biography of Alexander Hamilton.

We struck up a conversation about Hamilton and the Founding Fathers. The guy told me he was studying history at Swarthmore College and that he was most unhappy. He said he felt so suffocated by how doctrinaire thought life was on campus that he considered military service as an alternative for intellectual fresh air.

He said, "I'd prefer getting told what to *do* in an environment that's honestly disciplinarian, instead of getting told what to *think* in a college echo chamber that pretends to be 'liberal' but is actually close minded."

A few minutes later he thoughtfully added, "You know, your twenties can *really suck* when you feel pressured for them to be the best years of your life."

His words sparked a slew of memories from the prior twenty years and I understood precisely what he meant. So, I said, "Your twenties can be great if you embrace the suck and find ways to judo flip all the things bothering you, by using them to become a better man. Or even better yet, a *gentleman*."

Conclusion

I guess this ends the story. But not the journey. Some people said I should conclude by providing a list of recommendations for anyone interested in becoming a better gentleman. Although I wish we could boil everything down into such a list, I don't think it's possible.

As we saw at the beginning, the idea of the gentleman is fascinating and beautiful because it is *vague*. Most of it depends on sensibility and nuance. The only unassailable fixed rule worth following under all circumstances is the one from Jesus of Nazareth over two thousand years ago: "Love your neighbor as yourself."

Who can argue with that?

Beyond his general mandate, it's hard to get into detail. A gentleman blends two human traits which are inherently at odds with each other: excellence and equality. He seeks to be the smartest, strongest, toughest, most cultivated, and most compassionate guy he can be while always putting others above himself. He levels upward, not downward. He develops his personality in closely-knit groups where people spend "quantity time" together and have chance to get annoyed with each other and reach compromises through *conflict* and *forgiveness*.

In some cases, this conflict takes on a catty form of "passive aggression" where people are nice to your face and mean behind your back. Other times it's handled more bluntly, where friends are mean to your face and nice behind your back. Fisticuffs may occasionally be appropriate. But in every case, *grace* (a constant willingness to forgive both yourself and others) is the only social lubricant that allows everyone to make mistakes and *learn* from them.

My spur for wanting to become a better gentleman came from circumstances unique to me. Yours will come through circumstances unique to you. In my case, it came from growing up in a colonial-stock Pennsylvania family with a strong sense of history, with feminine influences from sisters at home and laddish influences from guys in sports and Boy Scouts (before that organization went co-ed) followed by university and military experiences in Millersville, Durham, Heidelberg, Fort Knox, Iraq, and Egypt.

These were my crucibles. Wherever you're from, you'll find your own crucibles and they will probably find you. I'm certain that every place on earth has groups in which iron sharpens iron and where people qualify as de facto ladies and gentlemen who demonstrate grace and excellence while leveling upward.

Gentlemanly character as I experienced it was only possible to develop through *conflict* when I was among challenging people with no easy "out." It occurred in romantic situations when women set high bars I couldn't always clear. It occurred in fraternal situations when male company forced me to become both rougher and more refined than I ever could have on my own. In each of these environments, there were never any "safe spaces" where viewpoints couldn't be shared just because they might cause offence.

Only through such conflict can your inner "delinquent male" get exposed and dealt with. This process best occurs when diversity of opinion is respected, and where people can't say "that offends me" as a clamp for shutting down dialogue.

Such freedom requires a pressure-release valve called HUMOR, a willingness to laugh things off, and to consider yourself the biggest joke of all.

Educationally, it's about holding scholastic aptitude in healthy contempt and embracing the idea that you don't need to earn "straight A's" in life's schools. Straight A's are only possible when you don't take risks that bring the chance to fail. By seeking uncomfortable situations in which your best efforts may only produce a string of "Gentleman's C's," you can rest in a hope that all those C's will add up to an A+ for overall gentlemanly character.

In addition to spending time with others, this process also requires solitude. By finding books worth reading, you just might find yourself doing things worth writing about. To paraphrase Kipling, if you occasionally make a heap of your winnings, risk it on one turn of pitch and toss, and lose, and start again at your beginnings, you may find that breaking down and crying is unavoidable. In such cases, writing things in a journal can work wonders. Journaling lets you work out your "issues" (we all have them) on paper—just as you'd figure out an algebra problem on scratch paper in math class.

American gentility is a gift from the ancient world, and more recently, from England. For centuries its standard bearers have been British, but in the twenty-first century it's an open door for anyone. When I think about the United States, and all the blessings and flaws we have as a diverse people, I see our two foundational documents, the Declaration of Independence and the Constitution, as an azimuth[51] for adapting the gentlemanly ideal for the future.

These documents reflect two dichotomies: individual freedom (Independence) on one hand and public responsibility (Constitution) on the

---

[51] An "azimuth" is a term from military land navigation that describes how a compass bearing accounts for where you have been and where you are going.

other. Together they form a carrot and stick. The Declaration encourages each of us to find happiness as individuals, the Constitution reins us in to share power through compromising with others.

As a teenager, I was more interested in the Independence side of this equation. After experiencing the older and more rigid cultures of England, Germany, and the military, I came to appreciate the Constitution as a model for restricting my own whims for the sake of others. Following this line of thought, gentlemanliness is best cultivated in organizations that provide equal measures of *freedom* (like the Declaration of Independence) and *discipline* (like the US Construction).

In each case unspoken "mores" (practical experience, habits, and opinions) are stronger than explicit rules. As Alexis de Tocqueville said, "I am convinced that even the most favorable geographical location and the best laws cannot maintain a constitution in spite of mores, whereas mores and even the most unfavorable locations and the worst laws to advantage."[52]

In 2019, some of our oldest institutions still reflect the mores of the ladies and gentlemen who founded them. In Philadelphia we have plenty of "ancient"

---

[52] Alexis de Tocqueville, *Democracy in America* (Library of America, New York, 2004).

(by American standards) establishments that quietly meet this description. But organizations have life cycles. Sometimes they get squelched through bureaucratization, disinterest, mission-drift, failure to adapt to new conditions, and over-eagerness to adopt new fads.

Regardless of how well such older organizations are faring, there's nothing more gentlemanly starting new ones from scratch. After all, that's what the Founding Fathers did when they formed the United States from a bunch of squabbling colonies; it's what original First City Troopers did when they converted their fox hunting club into a cavalry unit; it's what Endicott Peabody did when he launched the Groton School on Thomas Arnold's model at Rugby... and there are countless other examples.

If you can't find an iron-sharpening association of gentlemen to join, or if once-noble oaks are rotting from within, you can always gather some buddies, consider your values, and plant a new acorn today.

/

46557671R00102

Made in the USA
Middletown, DE
02 June 2019